MW00561638

SYSTEMS OF EVIL

A Study in Comparative Theodicy

Eric Odell-Hein

SYSTEMS OF EVIL

A Study in Comparative Theodicy

© 2017 by Eric Odell-Hein. All rights reserved.

Published by Redemption Press, PO Box 427, Enumclaw, WA 98022

Toll Free (844) 2REDEEM (273-3336)

Redemption Press is honored to present this title in partnership with the author. The views expressed or implied in this work are those of the author. Redemption Press provides our imprint seal representing design excellence, creative content, and high quality production.

No part of this publication may be reproduced, stored in a retrieval system, or transmitted in any way by any means—electronic, mechanical, photocopy, recording, or otherwise—without the prior permission of the copyright holder, except as provided by USA copyright law.

All Scripture quotations, unless otherwise indicated, are taken from the New American Standard Bible® (NASB), Copyright © 1960, 1962, 1963, 1968, 1971, 1972, 1973, 1975, 1977, 1995 by The Lockman Foundation. Used by permission. www.Lockman.org

ISBN 13: 978-1-68314-405-2 (Paperback)
978-1-68314-417-5 (Hard Cover)
978-1-68314-406-9 (ePub)
978-1-68314-407-6 (Mobi)

Library of Congress Catalog Card Number:

Acknowledgments

DR. RICK WALSTON WAS, as always, tireless in his reviews and offered excellent critiques. He has been a personal and academic mentor for many years, as well as a good friend. Rick proofed early versions of this study both early and often, and I thank him deeply.

Athena Dean Holtz from Redemption Press has been tremendously supportive. I heartily recommend authors investigate Redemption Press for their publishing needs.

Michelle Booth did a wonderful job of proofing and editing for publishing. This was my second time working with her, and she continues to be a great aid.

Thanks to the members of the Spurgeon-Lewis Consortium for their friendship, support, and tremendous theological discussions. Iron indeed sharpens iron. Dave, Dale, Marcus, Ross, John, Jay, and Doug have been great friends.

The Columbia Evangelical Seminary Board of Regents has been encouraging and supportive. Special thanks to Brent Atkison, Steve Rowe, Marcus Kelly, and Phil Fernandes.

Rev. Ross Holtz, the senior pastor of The Summit Evangelical Free Church in Enumclaw, WA, has been a nonstop supporter, friend, pastor, and mentor for me. Thank you, Ross.

Finally, many special thanks to my wife, Christine, who has patiently and steadfastly supported my research over the years.

Table of Contents

CHAPTER 1:

Introduction

THERE HAS BEEN SIGNIFICANT scholarly debate about the concept and problem of evil in recent times, particularly in religious circles. These efforts are commendable, as the whole idea of salvation must be precipitated by the crisis that evil evokes. In other words, if Christian believers are saved, from what is it that they are saved? Similarly, if Buddhist meditation liberates, then from what does it set its adherents free? Without such an understanding of the negative, then the positive becomes commensurately devoid of meaning. Moreover, any resultant personal commitment to a chosen belief system is thereby built on a tenuous foundation.

Dialogue between religious systems is often problematic, with no small part of the confusion being the result of different presuppositions, worldviews, and traditions (Bradley, 1955:34-37). The topic of evil can be challenging in this regard. In many ways, the combination of dogma and apology has served only to exacerbate the problem. There may also be acknowledged similarities between religious systems due to familiar terminology being employed, but without any qualifying definition, such perceived common ground can only foster further misunderstanding. For example, the Buddhist desire for deliverance from suffering might initially appear to parallel features of Christianity, though their underlying presuppositions (such as the doctrine of "no self") are entirely disparate and, therefore, ultimately incompatible (Das, 1998:119; Gethin, 1998:138-139). Many major religions struggle with communication because of misused terminology and misunderstood concepts. Indeed, the mainline forms of Hinduism, Islam, Judaism, Buddhism, and Christianity all offer much in the way of differing discourse on the topic, and so they will be examined in this book.

It is my conviction that for Christians to effectively communicate with non-Christians regarding the supremacy of God over evil and suffering, they must be well informed about the relationship between Christian theodicy and the explanations for evil and suffering found in other belief systems. A method is needed that provides a way to compare and classify such beliefs in such manner as to allow for direct and meaningful interfaith dialogue. Interfaith dialogue in no ways implies a universal, inclusive, or syncretistic view of the world's religions. Rather, proper interfaith dialogue acknowledges many differences between religions, some of which are fundamental and antithetical to other belief systems. In acknowledging these differences, interfaith dialogue seeks to establish proper conceptual understanding and terminological equivalence for the sake of broad comprehension and acknowledgment of differences.

As yet, there seems to have been no purposeful attempt to furnish a satisfactory, comprehensive, and methodical comparison of beliefs that covers the theological, philosophical, and experiential approaches an individual must consider when evaluating the problem of evil. It may come as no surprise that many of the writings on the topic of evil are not only specific to one particular religious system, but they are also similarly limited in their analytical execution. This can be seen in differences in mainstream approaches to Buddhism (cf. Radhakrishnan and Moore,

1999; Chodron, 2000; Goleman, 2003) as well as within the Christian mainstream, where the approaches taken include the personal (Lewis, 2001), the philosophical (Geisler, 2002) and the purely theological (Wright, 2006). Judaism (Al-Fayyūmī, 1998; Carmy, 1999) and Islam (Ali, 1990) are also well represented without providing much by way of material that encourages dialogue. As such, the studies available do not adequately afford aid to understanding the core issues in the major systems of religious thought regarding evil in such a way as to provide a channel for discussing them in a universal fashion. This oversight will be addressed herein.

A Christian who engages in interfaith dialogue on the topic of evil must be able to operate within an established frame that identifies the key components of various faiths as well as points of contrast and comparison. That person must not be predisposed to favor or disadvantage any participating belief system. This book proposes a system that facilitates effective interfaith dialogue on theodicy regardless of the faith of the participant. Furthermore, this book proposes a new Christian paradigm that works within the proposed system to effectively display the uniqueness and sufficiency of the Christian approach to the problem of evil when engaged in the interfaith dialogue.

The variety within each religion presents additional challenges since any comparative study must define the scope of work with regard to inclusion or exclusion of specific expressions of each faith. With that in mind, this approach will focus on mainstream forms of each religion. For the theistic faiths, Judaism will be studied from Steinberg's definition of the traditional perspective (strict traditional and modernist-traditional) as opposed to fully modern or mystical perspectives (1975:10). Christianity will be analyzed from mainstream Protestant views. The Islamic portion of this book will proceed from mainline Sunni views as they represent the vast majority of the world's Islamic population (Farah, 2003:174; Gordon, 2003:92; Renard, 2002:214; Smith, 1991:258). Within Sunni

Islam, the moderate, modern forms, as defined by Danheisser (2003), will be considered, as opposed to radical, fundamentalist Islam. When examining the varieties of Buddhism, the focus will be on the general teachings of the Theravada and Mahayana traditions, while localized or syncretistic expressions necessitate exclusion from this study. Hinduism remains a challenge for scholars to define, and this analysis will employ Michaels' classification of Hindu belief systems (2004:20-22). The closest identifiable equivalent to mainstream Hindu religious form is the Brahmanic-Sanskritic classification, although tribal and folk expressions of Hinduism that fall in line with Brahmanic-Sanskritic practices (with only non-heretical deviances) will also be included in this study. Founded religions with a Hindu origin that subsequently distinguished themselves from Hinduism, such as Jainism, Buddhism, and Sikhism, are not part of mainline Hinduism, and they will be excluded from the Hindu portion of this study.

The Focus of This Study

The central research question of this work, therefore, is: "How may one frame and conduct effective interfaith dialogue about evil, and how may the uniqueness and sufficiency of the Christian understanding of evil be presented from within the context of that framework?"

The questions that naturally emerge from this problem are:

- ➢ What meaningful information may be gleaned by conducting a critical examination of existing works in mainline Judaism, Christianity, Islam, Hinduism, and Buddhism regarding the concept of evil and, thereby, determining each individual definition of evil (or its equivalent)?
- ➢ What are the key questions and the theological, philosophical, and experiential components addressed by each belief system?

- ➢ What kind of universal code of classification and identification for religious thought about evil could be created?
- ➢ How can the mainline expressions of the major religious belief systems of Hinduism, Buddhism, Islam, Judaism, and Christianity be classified according to the newly created code?
- ➢ What conclusions may be thereby deduced about the sufficiency and uniqueness of the Christian paradigm regarding the concept of evil in support of its claim to exclusive truth and sufficiency?

The aim of this book is to provide a framework for effective interfaith communication and understanding regarding the concept of evil and to provide a Christian paradigm that operates within this framework to demonstrate the uniqueness and sufficiency of the Christian approach to evil.

This theological study will employ in-depth critical literary research of textual works that explain the various belief systems. It will be an evaluative analysis of the appropriate literary contributions in order to discern each religion's core theological positions with regard to evil and suffering. It will be first an assessment of the collated data. Second, it will present that information in a juxtaposed topical classification for easy comparison. Finally, it will identify the consistencies and inconsistencies as well as the strengths and weaknesses of the positions of each of the major religious belief systems under investigation.

The methodology to be employed for the evaluative analysis will be twofold: first, all reviews of each religion's literature will be seen through the grammatical-historical principle of hermeneutics (i.e., the Single-Meaning principle). In brief, this study will take the writings at face value and not impose foreign ideas into their meanings. Second, this work will employ the consistent use of basic philosophical laws of thought (e.g., law of identity, law of non-contradiction, and law of excluded middle) as appropriate. The infrastructure of each view is dependent upon logical (consistent) stability. Each view can be judged as consistent or inconsistent through the assessment of its logical coherence. Applying the basic laws of philosophical thought, one can objectively assess these various positions as well as compare and contrast them one against the other.

Many studies have already presented arguments for differing Christian approaches to reconciling evil and human suffering with the goodness of God. Since several quality works are already available on that topic, this study seeks to cover new ground primarily regarding comparative theodicy. As such, a student of theodicy who is accustomed to reading detailed philosophical examinations of common Christian positions will note the lack of such herein. Rather, this work seeks to meet a need heretofore unmet in a satisfactory manner.

The Concept of Evil in the World's Major Religions

The concept of evil is familiar to most people. Definitions of right and wrong exist in all societies, and occasions of human suffering are prevalent throughout history. Natural occurrences, such as the tsunami that struck parts of southeast Asia in 2004 or Hurricane Katrina, which brought devastation and grief to large parts of the United States Gulf Coast in 2005, provide potent examples of suffering. This severe suffering can cause people to question the nature of the universe and the basic goodness, or lack thereof, of any supposed supernatural deities. When faced with suffering and undesirable circumstances that seem to be undeserved, people tend to examine the nature of the interaction between the Divine and humanity. Horrific events precipitated by human will and action also lead people to question the nature of the Divine as well as the intrinsic nature of humanity itself. The Holocaust, Stalin's purges, and the Rwandan genocide are a few examples of the horrors that have provided the last few generations with much to ponder in this regard. However, when it comes to creating a definition of evil, people from the various mainstream expressions of the major religions agree on precious little.

The first step in this study is to discern and define a broad approach to the concept and definition of evil that can encompass the various nuances of each underlying worldview of the major religious systems covered in this study. In the general sense of the word evil, it is appropriate to account for a variety of perspectives that include seemingly innocent human suffering, moral depravity, sin, and other items in this thematic vein. However, one can view these concepts in such way as to presuppose a worldview that favors absolutes, such as in theism, in which it is possible to define good and evil as antithetical concepts. When attempting to make accurate use of the antithetical definition, non-theistic religious systems, such as Buddhism or Hinduism, have more challenges, and so many of these concepts do not easily fit into those systems. Along those lines, how should one approach defining evil in a manner that can include these other views?

The key to solving this lies with a religious system's definition of goodness or the ultimate goal. While a pure concept of evil (as in a traditionally theistic sense) may be conspicuous in its seeming absence in some religious systems, its equivalent may still be discerned by a careful analysis of those things that may be considered the most opposite of good in a particular system of religious thought. Likewise, if there is something that commonly prevents an individual from achieving the greatest possible good as defined by that religious system, one should consider it when identifying a particular concept of evil. Because of the importance given to human experiences of evil and suffering, it will also be clear that the perceived sources of human suffering are vital components of the concept of evil when engaged in comparative study.

With that in mind, analysis of each religious system under consideration in this book begins. The first step is to engage varied, authoritative sources—with a heavy emphasis on native sources—in order to discern how each particular mainstream expression of the major religious systems define evil (keeping in mind the broad considerations just put forth). The second step is to carefully balance the views of the various patterns of religious thought present within each particular system. As mentioned earlier, this study will focus on the mainstream forms of each religious system under consideration. For example, when dealing with a religion such as Judaism that has a wide variety of traditions covering ultra-orthodox, modern, liberal, mystical, and many others, the expressions of faith that lie outside the mainstream will not play a major role in this study. Even with this limited scope of investigation, there is a variety of mainstream expressions within each faith, and by engaging with these various, distinctive traditions a clear picture of the overall form of the concept of evil emerges. After the initial analysis of the concept of evil for each of the five religious systems is complete, the book will advance to a deeper, topical analysis of each concept in a new chapter.

CHAPTER 2:

The Concept of Evil in Judaism

The Approach to Evil in Judaism

JUDAISM HAS A LONG tradition of grappling with the concept of evil and suffering. This tradition stretches from its canonically earliest scriptures (Genesis 3), through the speculations of Job and his friends on evil, suffering, and the justice of God, and into contributions of the Talmud (Cohen, 1995; Elman, 1990). It also shows itself in the Middle Ages (Al-Fayyumi, 1998) as well as in the last century (Carmy, 1999; Lichtenstein, 1999; Brener, 2004; Fackenheim, 1985). Perhaps more than other religions, Judaism identifies itself very closely with the actual life experiences of its adherents, and that serves to amplify the personal experiences of evil and to create a central role for those experiences in the discussion of theodicy. When one combines these experiences with deep philosophical considerations and a strong theological tradition, the concept of evil in Judaism emerges.

The debate about evil plays a significant role in Judaism. However, delving into this topic immediately brings some difficulties to the fore. There is a significant strain of thought in Judaism (even in the mainstream) that avoids dealing with the topic of evil or at least acknowledges a sense of impropriety when doing so. This apparent conflict can be seen in the Talmudic tradition, which still holds great sway on mainstream Judaism. The writings in the Palestinian Talmud minimize the occurrence and importance of evil, but the writings that comprise the Babylonian Talmud engage with this topic in thorough fashion (Elman, 1990:315-339). Building on the seeming reluctance of the Palestinian Talmudic tradition to embrace this theme, some prominent commentators and writers offer a variety of views that could be considered apprehensive approaches to the topic of evil and God. These views claim that God made evil as something that may be beyond human comprehension (Goodman, 1998:94), or that theodicy has been of little apparent relevance in the lives of adherents (Sokol, 1999:312). Another author writes of Judaism's focus on people making themselves better and more worthy instead of worrying about evil or suffering (Steinberg, 1975:56-57, 87). Still another author relates that speculation on the nature of evil may be misguided and that one ought to work on performing good deeds (Carmy, 1999:11). Even the Kaddish (a common Jewish prayer that adherents ritually recite at the burial of a body) does not dwell on loss or raise questions about the seeming injustice of a life that has ended; rather, it speaks boldly of God's glory and majesty (Brener, 2004:84-85). The underlying implication is that humankind need not worry about why things happen; rather, people should move on and perhaps perform good deeds to make things better. However, these views, if one accepts them as fully accurate, appear to stand in direct opposition to both human nature and general religious traditions throughout the world. It appears contradictory to claim the existence of an immanent, good, caring God who allows people to suffer without explanation. Perceiving a failure to understand and address the problem of evil, others from outside the faith could incorrectly perceive the nature of Judaism's God as cruelly indifferent, or they could also view its adherents as choosing a path of blind faith in a sadistic deity.

Even though there is seeming reluctance to engage with the topic by some Jewish sources, the search for explanations for the reality of evil, the prosperity of the wicked, and the suffering of the innocent, has consistently been part of human religion, and in the end Judaism is no exception once all the sources are carefully weighed and considered. In lending support to the need to engage with this topic, some prominent authors describe evil and suffering as one of the most fundamental questions Judaism must face (Goodman, 1998:29; Ariel, 1995:101). This is particularly evident given last century's Holocaust and the need to understand God's promises in the Torah in relation to the terrible suffering the Nazi regime inflicted on the Jews (Heschel, 1976:421).

Judaism's theistic view of the universe teaches that humankind is subordinate and inferior to the one, true God. Unlike Eastern religious systems that teach divinity is found within each individual as an intrinsic part of one's true self, Judaic theology (an expression of the theistic worldview) teaches that God is separate from (though still involved with) and superior to humanity. Thus, there is severe reluctance to do anything that might incorrectly represent or unintentionally blaspheme God. Blasphemy is a terrible transgression, as evidenced by Talmudic Judaism, which taught that there was no forgiveness for a person who profaned the name of God (Cohen, 1995:23). With this in mind, it is easy to understand how a tradition of non-engagement could develop out of a combination of deep respect and significant fear. Christian scriptures relate an incident where the Pharisees attempted to stone Jesus for apparently claiming to be God. They considered this to be a profanation of His holy name, which earned the accused blasphemer death (John 8:52-59). Their desire to stone Jesus demonstrated the severity of the perceived sin.

All forms of Judaism strongly proclaim the goodness of God from the outset, and no one wants to call that into question, even if it is unintentional. Therefore, while there is seeming reluctance on the part of some writers to engage with the topic of evil and to question why the wicked prosper and the innocent suffer (Sokol, 1999:312; Carmy, 1999:11) this is not indicative of a lack of concern on the part of the faithful. Rather, it is evidence of Judaism's reverence for the supremacy and holiness of God as well as its fear of inadvertently profaning Him by using finite, human thought to classify and judge the workings of the infinite, holy God. Nevertheless, a large volume of material in Judaism deals with evil and with how the goodness of God plays an important—and theologically difficult—role in Judaism's formulation of the concept of evil (Al-Fayyumi, 1998; Ariel, 1995; Cohen, 1995; Heschel, 1976; Brener, 2004; Satlow, 2003; Steinberg, 1975).

Even with some reluctance to engage too deeply with the topic, Judaism acknowledges evil as real, strong, and tempting, and one can often see evidence of it in the experiential form of human suffering (Goodman, 1998:29; Heschel, 1976:369). This suffering naturally drives people to ask questions as to why evil exists, and if it exists, to question whether God is truly good and powerful. Despite restraint shown in this area by some authors, Lytton offers a powerful argument for the accountability of God in the Jewish scriptures. In analyzing God's interaction with Abraham preceding His judgment of Sodom and Gomorrah, Lytton describes God's willingness to be visible and accountable for how He judges Sodom and Gomorrah. The Hebrew term used there, *vayashkifu*, implies seeing (or judging) while being seen (or judged) at the same time. God is judging Sodom while Abraham is watching and forming opinions about God's justice at the same time (2002:46-47).

If this argument is accepted, it allows for an honest, respectful, and non-profaning examination of Jewish theodicy. Al-Fayyumi's commentary on Job appears to imply some amount of agreement on this topic. He wrote that for Job to refrain from offering an opinion on God's justice—to refrain for any reason at all including humility—would be equivalent to an implicit condemnation of God and of His justice. While he did not believe that humans could fully comprehend evil, he did believe that in the conversation between God and Job, God's engagement with Job and the fullness of evidence presented to Job created a situation that *demanded positive judgment* by the human participant. His conclusion was that not offering judgment was as much a profanation of God's name as if one made a judgment that explicitly declared God to be unjust (1998:408-409). Talmudic traditions also painstakingly declared God to be both justice and mercy (Cohen, 1995:17, 110, 116), and the Babylonian portion of the Talmud engages extensively with this topic (Elman, 1990:315-339). The *keriah*, a mourning ritual that involves tearing a cloth to reflect one's anger and disappointment during bereavement, provides further evidence of the Judaic belief in the goodness of God: as one performs the ritual of pain and loss, a verbal recitation that acknowledges God's justice is also performed (Brener, 2004:113-116).

From a collective, critical look at the various views, including biblical evidence, theological commentary, rabbinic traditions, common rituals, and historical consistency, it appears that people are to examine God against their personal experiences of evil and suffering so long as they declare Him just. Therefore, it is not only proper to examine evil in Judaism, but it is a core theological position that God is good, just, and that people must declare Him as such.

When one attempts to fully understand the concept of evil in Judaism, one should note that the Holocaust has significantly influenced Jewish theodicy. Some people, considering the impact of the Holocaust, discern a new, "radical" embodiment of evil: internalized idolatry leading to new depths of evil action that previous Jewish philosophy did not adequately address (Fackenheim, 1985:505-514; McRobert, 1989:332-333). Jonas echoes this view. He describes the Holocaust as something that pre-existing Jewish theodicies cannot categorize because of its very nature (1987:3). Others acknowledge a degree of validity in the desire to define the Holocaust as a radical evil; however, others also argue that the concept of radical evil has taken on a life of its own and is no longer consistent within the context of the Holocaust (Betts, 2002:544). In contrast to these views of radical evil, other Jewish adherents voice full confidence in the ability of pre-existing theodicies to account for the Holocaust. Neusner claims other notable representatives of Judaism, such as Rubenstein and Fackenheim, harm Judaism and the faith of Jewish believers when they seek for new explanations that lie outside the traditional forms (1973:307). For Neusner, as for many others, the classic forms of Judaism have always been sufficient, and they continue to be sufficient even for something as horrible as the Holocaust (1973:307). Others also present the Holocaust as mere perpetual banality when individual actions and accountability are carefully considered (Mathewes, 2000:390-392). Clearly, there is serious disagreement, even in mainstream Judaism, as to how to view the Holocaust in terms of its fundamentally evil nature. Regardless of the disagreements, post-World War II theodicy has been dramatically impacted by the Holocaust, and Judaism is still struggling to reconcile its various concepts of evil accordingly. This will be evident in any study of Jewish sources from the last sixty years, and it merits acknowledgment and consideration in this book, as some of these variations will be evident.

Evil as an Internal Impulse

When starting to examine evil in Judaism, it is important to address the absence of original sin in Jewish theology, particularly if one is addressing an audience with a background in Christian thought. Jewish theology considers the disobedience of Adam in Genesis to be a sinful act, but Judaic thought does not indicate that his offspring were inherently sinful and unable to please God; there is no corrupted human nature resulting from this original sin (Cohen, 1995:96; Ariel,

1995:84-85). This doctrine is a core part of Jewish theology, even though Jewish sources generally expect that a person's life will indeed contain some sin (Steinberg, 1975:89). While rabbis sometimes disagreed on if a person could hypothetically live a truly sinless life (Cohen, 1995:95), an analysis of Jewish writings indicates that individuals will most likely commit several sins during their lifetimes (Steinberg, 1975:89; Heschel, 1976:393; Ariel, 1995:91). Declarations of individuals as having lived a sinless life are rare, and they are not necessarily accepted as fact by most of the mainstream. While an individual does not inherit a sinful nature from his or her ancestors, it is important to note that some consequences of sin (in the form of suffering and circumstances) do indeed have their source in the evil acts of an ancestor (Ariel, 1995:102). Likewise, God might dole out some grace to a specific individual due to the meritorious actions of an ancestor who found favor with God (Ariel, 1995:101; Cohen, 1995:96). However, one should note that inherited evil consequences do not equate to an inherited sinful nature, and the possibility of an individual to live a sinless life (however unlikely and possibly never actualized) points to the lack of a sinful nature in humanity. Judaism is very distinct—and explicitly so—from Christianity in this aspect of theology. Humankind does not have a dominant sinful nature, and humankind is completely able to please God via actions even though people sin (Ehrlich, 2003:38; Ariel, 1995:84-85, 91; Cohen, 1995:96; Heschel, 1976:374-378).

However, this lack of an inherited, sinful nature does not imply that people are not inclined to sin. Rather, Judaism teaches that there are two impulses resident within every human being: one impulse leads people to perform good deeds, and the other impulse leads people to commit evil deeds. Talmudic writings confirm that God did indeed create both impulses (Cohen, 1995:39, 88). Rabbis defended this position by noting that the story of creation uses the word *wajjitzer*, which means "and He formed." The use of two "j"s indicated to them that God created both urges (Cohen, 1995:88). One rabbinic commentary claims evidence of this view by citing God's creation of two things present in the Garden of Eden: The Tree of the Knowledge of Good and Evil and the tempting serpent are evidence of the impulse (Scherman & Zlotowitz, 1999:12, 15).

When it comes to the evil impulse and its effects, keeping in mind that the impulse is from God, it becomes theologically awkward to resolve the apparent conflict between the doctrine of divine benevolence and the topics of death, suffering, and the evil impulse itself. Jewish theology handles this by simply restating, with limited justification, that the evil impulse falls under the doctrine that everything created by God must either be of benefit or serve to glorify Him (Cohen, 1995:39-40; Heschel, 1976:415). The natures of the two impulses differ significantly. The good impulse is generally passive and does not drive people toward action, while the evil impulse is more active, and it contains the necessary energy that drives people to do things. This is where the justification for the evil impulse shows up. Without the energy of the evil impulse, many of the acts necessary for human existence would not take place, such as conducting business, creating a home, marrying a wife, and having children (Satlow, 2003:209-210; Ariel, 1995:86-87; Cohen, 1995:90; Heschel, 1976:415). In these views, the concept of evil teaches that God places urge, energy, and temptation within people in order to serve His plan, even though the nature and power of the evil impulse naturally leads people toward acts of true evil (Heschel, 1976:365; Ariel, 1995:86). God also provides the significantly less powerful good impulse as a counterbalance, and the expectation is that people will harness the good impulse, along with the Torah, to channel the necessary energies of the evil impulse toward non-evil ends (Cohen, 1995:91-92; Heschel, 1976:375; Steinberg, 1975:87).

Evil as Human Action

Sources clearly indicate that every individual needs to try to conquer, subdue, or channel the energy of the evil impulse away from those things that are bad (its natural inclination) and toward good actions. If someone chooses to use the evil impulse to commit evil, then it begins a downward spiral from which it is difficult to recover. The evil urge grows stronger within people as it is used, and God punishes the individuals who indulge the evil impulse by helping them follow the evil path they have chosen (Satlow, 2003:217; Cohen, 1995:91-95; Heschel, 1976:377). However, God's aid is reactive and not prescriptive. God predetermines many circumstances of an individual's life: the time of an individual's birth, one's station in life, health, prosperity, wisdom, and more. However, while God in His omniscience knows who will choose to follow evil and who will choose to do good, He does not predetermine those choices for the individuals (Cohen, 1995:11-14, 93-94). When individuals make free-will choices to engage their evil impulse for bad deeds instead of good, then those evil choices are actualized as evil actions, and God helps those people to continue in their descent (Cohen, 1995:94-95).

While the writings of Judaism often talk about the evil impulse, these writings give greater weight to the choices made by an individual in providing the most visible, measurable concept of good and evil. One can discern the importance of an individual's deeds by sampling a variety of common beliefs. For example, if someone commits an evil act against another person, it is as if that evil act was committed directly against God. This is a worse offense if it is committed against a Gentile. In this scenario, the evil act bears evil witness against God, and is a profanation of His name in front of one who is an unbeliever (Cohen, 1995:23, 101). Good deeds could serve to improve the person performing the deed, provide some measure of spiritual cleansing, and earn merit toward redemption in the eyes of God (Ben-Menahem, 2002:22; Ariel, 1995:159; Heschel, 1976:377; Steinberg, 1975:35-36).

The determination of a deed as good or evil necessitates an external authority. This external authority enables one to make these value judgments. In Judaism that authority is God, and Judaism makes it clear that His will and plan for humanity is divinely revealed in the Torah. The word "Torah" often means guidance, teaching, or doctrine (Steinberg, 1975:21-22). In collective terms, the Torah represents the core teachings of Judaism as the Jews best understood and practiced them, and as such, it evolves and changes as humans interpret it according to their views and circumstances. Even though different expressions of the Jewish faith interpret sections or commandments differently, the foundational nature of the Torah remains consistent. It is God's will expressed to humanity and further interpreted for human guidance. Many describe Judaism as humankind engaging with God *and with the Torah*, and even though interpretations differ, the Torah remains a central, binding component of mainstream Jewish thought (Ben-Menahem, 2002:22-28; Benatar, 2002:10-11; Dozeman, 2000:29).

The actual role of the Torah in determining which actions are right and wrong appears to change depending on the expression of Judaism one practices; therefore, understanding the various perspectives of the Torah is vital before additional analysis can begin. Traditional Judaism tends to interpret the Torah literally, and in doing so, there is less allowance given for the modernization of the extracted precepts to account for changing social and political climates. This would include several orthodox expressions (Ariel, 1995:135). Traditional forms are the most historically consistent and recognizable expressions of Judaism, and they remain part of the mainstream expression of the faith. Modernist expressions of Judaism tend to view the Torah as true and authoritative insofar as it matches the human criteria of experience and reason (Steinberg, 1975:27). In these circles, there is allowance in the interpretation of the Torah to account for modern, changing times and evolving social situations (Spero, 1986:79-90). Regardless of the traditional or modern approaches to Judaism, if individuals engage their impulses to follow a commandment of the Torah, the resultant deeds are good. When someone is tempted to do evil but is able to resist, it is also good. The acts that conform to the expressed will of God are mitvot. However, when one does something that the Torah prohibits, the evil act is an averah (plural is averot). This closely equates with the concept of sin in other theistic religions. Averot are not limited to actions that do not properly conform to the guidance of the Torah. Nonaction when good action or resistance is called for is also evil or averah (Feldman, 2000:281).

Regarding the impact of averot, Judaism teaches that evil acts do not make an individual intrinsically flawed or unable to please God via his or her own actions. The existence and central importance of the Torah is evidence of this. If humans were incapable of sufficiently following the Torah, God would not have provided it. By having the Torah to follow, Judaism has a guide by which to work toward gradually improving oneself and living a life that contains more good deeds than evil, but not necessarily a life that is completely void of evil deeds (Ben-Menahem, 2002:22-23; Ariel, 1995:91; Heschel, 1976:393). Therefore, all people are required to do good deeds. Evil exists when a person who can please God by following the Torah and performing good deeds does not do so (Steinberg, 1975:86; Cohen, 1995:96).

Evil as the External Influence of Satan and Evil Spirits

The supernatural realm is also a place where evil exists. Satan and other evil spirits are evil. As with the evil impulse, Satan and evil spirits are part of God's purpose and divine plan. Satan and evil spirits are instruments of temptation and punishment that God created for His specific purposes (Heschel, 1976:370; Cohen 1995:54-57). It may be helpful to think of the evil impulse as the internal drive for evil, while Satan and evil spirits are the external drive for evil. Judaic writings also indicate that evil spirits can possess people and cause them to commit acts of evil (Cohen, 1995:260). These acts of possession are not necessarily direct expressions of God's divine wrath or of His punishment. Rather, it appears that evil spirits have enough will of their own to possess vulnerable individuals and cause them to sin (Cohen, 1995:260). The Judaic views of Satan and evil spirits show the role of evil spirits in relation to the concept of evil, though it is the least-emphasized component in the full system of evil.

Evil and Suffering as Consequential Circumstances or the Result of Deeds

Actions that do not conform to the Torah lead to another discernible aspect of evil in Judaism: when the evil urge becomes manifest in evil actions, those evil actions bring suffering to individuals and to the world. The experiential consequences of evil actions are important to include in this study. Suffering is a vital, experiential component of evil in Judaism, and suffering is sometimes considered to be the only way for humans to measure evil in the world since it is observable and physical (Ariel, 1995:101). Both personal and widespread suffering results from acts of evil, including the suffering of those who appear to be innocent. One's own averot may lead directly to one's own individual experience of suffering. If someone experiences an affliction to their sight (such as blindness), then that can be a direct result of a sin of the eyes (Cohen, 1995:111, 116). Collective averot may lead to collective suffering. The departure of the *Shekinah*, which means the glory or presence of God, leads to widespread suffering and evil in the world. This departure occurs as a direct result of people's sins and arrogance (Cohen, 1995:44-45, 216). Widespread, generational evil deeds produce circumstances where evil and suffering are stronger and more pervasive than goodness. This is closer to modernist views as it embraces a more figurative concept of the presence of God and the arrival of the Messiah, placing an emphasis on the requirement of collective human goodness (Steinberg, 1975:170). While Judaic thought offers differing explanations for suffering and the justification of God, they all proclaim the fairness of God, the sin of people, and the justice of rewards (Lichtenstein, 1999:40-41; Cohen, 1995:117-118; Heschel 1976; 364).

Summary of Judaism's Concept of Evil

When one analyzes the sources in Judaism, a clear picture of evil emerges. Whether the individual expression of faith leans more toward the traditional or modern, mainstream Judaism teaches that God has a plan for humanity. People can engage with His plan via the Torah, and humans can live righteously according to the Torah. Evil exists to some extent in the evil impulse within people, and it also exists as a spiritual influence coming from Satan and evil spirits; however, a large part of the definition of evil is provided by the actions people take that are not in accordance with the Torah. These nonconforming actions result in suffering. The resultant suffering plays a large role in Jewish tradition and regarding evil. This deep tradition of evil is a pattern that is familiar to both traditional and modern Judaism, and it is what all its adherents strive to conquer.

CHAPTER 3:

The Concept of Evil in Christianity

Christianity's Differentiation

CHRISTIANITY HAS TRADITIONALLY DIFFERENTIATED itself from much of Judaic thought by way of interpretation and theology even though it shares approximately two-thirds of its scriptures with Judaism. One ought not to ignore or marginalize the common, shared heritage of scripture. However, there are significant differences. God incarnate as a human is a new theological development, as is Jesus' claim to be the Messiah. His subsequent sacrifice, bodily resurrection, and eternal reign continue these differences, and this leads to a very different interpretation of the shared scriptures. In accordance with that, there are vast theological differences between the Judaic thought and the theologies put forth in the New Testament. Christianity likewise is differentiated from Islam in many of these same areas of theology, despite Islamic claims of Jesus as a prophet and Christianity as a "Religion of the Book."

As with the other theistic faiths, Christianity struggles diligently with the problem of evil, but the solution offered is markedly distinct in most areas, and Judaism and Islam end up being far more like each other than they are to Christianity, at least regarding their theodicies. These differences come in a few key areas. To start with, the concept of the nature of evil is unique in Christian thought, and the effect of sin and evil on human nature is different. This necessarily leads to further differentiation in how Christianity approaches evil and its defeat, and Christ's incarnation adds further points of difference.

While other religions also have differing sects and variations, the variety found in Christian denominations is also multitudinous. While some differences may be relatively minor (Assemblies of God compared to the Foursquare Church, for example), other differences within the Christian community are significant. The first step in this portion of the study is to identify what comprises mainstream, biblical Christianity. Some varieties that publicly claim to be part of the Christian faith are easy to exclude from this study. The Church of Jesus Christ of Latter-Day Saints (Mormonism) along with the Jehovah's Witness and the Watchtower Bible and Tract Society (Jehovah's Witnesses) deny the doctrine of the Trinity and are therefore not actually Christian according to the orthodox beliefs of the mainline expressions of Christianity (and are therefore excluded). The Seventh Day Adventists are often classified as an outlying Christian sect (and earlier in its history as an outright cult) with some heterodox beliefs (Martin, W., 2003: 535-627). Nevertheless, they still fall outside of what is part of the mainstream expression of the Christian faith; therefore, the doctrines offered by the General Conference of the Seventh Day Adventist Church are excluded from participation in this study.

Many other expressions do indeed fall under the heading of mainstream Protestant Christianity. Lutheran, Baptist, Nazarene, Evangelical Free, Assemblies of God, Foursquare, Presbyterian, and others may differ severely and with great conviction on specific points of theology or practice; yet regarding the topic of evil, they have much in common.

Difficulties can arise out of specific views taken on certain theological topics that are not always consistent within denominational bounds. For example, the Evangelical Free Church of America does not regulate or promote any specific view such as extreme Calvinism, moderate Calvinism, Molinism, or Arminianism, instead choosing to emphasize more basic, common doctrines (*Statement of Faith*, 2008). The claim that some approaches to specific aspects of theology represent *the* mainstream Christian viewpoint is difficult to establish, and in the end, all of them combined better represent mainstream Protestant Christianity. For example, in response to James White's critique (White, 2000) of Geisler's approach to soteriology, Geisler acknowledges the differences between his approach to soteriology and James White's approach (Geisler, 2001:252-263). As evidence that these differences do not cause deviation from the accepted mainstream, Geisler gently chides White for his fervent attack and writes that White's efforts would be better spent channelling his talents and efforts toward defending Christianity from attacks that come against it as opposed to engaging those that share the faith (Geisler, 2001:263). While there are some differences in the approach taken to the problem of evil by each of the Christian viewpoints in this study, one should remember that the focus of this study is on the general system of thought about evil, not the specific details within each participating faith system. In other words, there is a general, mainstream Christian view on evil that all various expressions of the mainstream Christian faith generally share. Some extreme versions of the above viewpoints may go so far as to have a system-altering perspective, but extreme expressions lie outside the mainstream and are excluded from this study.

Open Theism merits special attention as it presents a challenge for the Christian portion of this study. Over the past few decades, Open Theism has been gaining followers in Christian circles (including some churches that most would generally consider part of mainstream denominations). Though considered by many theologians to be outside traditional orthodoxy (Ware, 2000; Frame, 2001; Helseth, 2001), its enthusiastic followers have wielded much popular influence. The attacks made by traditionally orthodox theologians vary in style and effectiveness, though not in passion. Open Theism is of special interest in this study not just because of its recent surge in popularity, but because of its large focus on the problem of evil and the impact it has on modern, popular approaches to theodicy.

Some crusaders against Open Theism, such as Ware (2000) and Frame (2001), are enthusiastic defenders of the traditional theistic views of Christianity. However, when dealing specifically with the problem of evil, and particularly when faced with the sticky question of foreknowledge and predestination, their arguments focus on the worst possible interpretations offered by Open Theists, and their positions ignore the more subtle, complex answers offered in the middle ground by traditional theists such as Geisler (2002:31). Frame lumps together Arminians, Open Theists, and even many moderate Calvinists (perhaps unintentionally) when discussing the issue (2001:135-136), which is an oversimplification (and possibly offensive to many who are lumped into this attack but who do not endorse Open Theism). Ware uses a straw-man tactic when he postulates what an Open Theist *might* say, writing a long paragraph that supposedly verbalizes that straw-man perspective and then attacks it based on the words he has just written on their behalf (Ware, 2000:199-200). These poor approaches to a difficult topic overlook the occasionally eloquent elucidations of the problem of evil facing Christianity. By contrast, Helseth critiques the Open Theist views (of Boyd in particular) in a manner that avoids polemic bludgeoning and emphasizes scholarly consistency in approach and application, something which he notes is lacking in Boyd's views (2001:497-510). Helseth's scholarly approach allows for precision in critique as well as constructive evaluation of any potentially valuable viewpoints brought up in the theological disagreement. This provides a guide for how this study will deal with the appropriate level of inclusion of Open Theism.

With that in mind, this study will take the following approach to Open Theism: as it falls outside of traditional Christian orthodoxy, which still constitutes the majority—though not the entirety—of mainstream Christianity, many of the Open Theistic views will generally fall outside of the purview of this study. However, as Open Theism has much to say on the problem of evil, and while it does play some role in shaping the modern mainstream discussions, this study will not wholly exclude its viewpoints. Rather, the portions of thought expressed by Open Theists that do not appear to fall outside of the bounds of traditional orthodoxy (as expressed by many of the other, more traditional theologians cited in this section) will be included. To that end, this work cites some well-known Open Theists, such as Pinnock and Boyd.

This falls in line with the overall source approach to this topic. Since the author of this study comes from one of the mainstream, orthodox expressions of the Christian faith mentioned earlier, care must be taken not to give inordinate weight to the viewpoints from his background. To that end special care has been taken to include a broad representation of mainstream, orthodox Christianity when conducting this portion of the study. As a result of this approach, the sources cited come from a mix of backgrounds and include strong and moderate Calvinism, Molinism, and Arminianism. It also includes representation from several different denominations, experts in a variety of disciplines (apologetics, systematic theology, philosophy, philosophy of religion, Christian bio-ethics), and even a couple of highly influential theologians who lived and wrote prior to the Reformation (Augustine and Aquinas). Regardless of differences in the details offered by each individual or expression, the overall system of evil in mainstream Christianity is consistent and emerges intact.

Defining Metaphysical Evil

The dilemma facing Judaism regarding God's goodness and His creation of the evil impulse is something that could have posed a similar challenge to Christianity. In addition, dualistic thinking was a force to be reckoned with during the early stages of Christianity. It was during these early stages of the development of Christian theology that Augustine eloquently laid out the philosophy for metaphysical evil that would guide much of Christian thought on the topic through to modern times. A careful look at Augustine's writings in Book VII of *Confessions* shows that he was acutely aware of the type of dilemma facing the Judaic thinkers (God is good, so He could not have created anything evil, e.g., the evil impulse) as well as the dualism of the Manicheans (Augustine, 1961:133-156). Augustine's first step was to reinforce the concept of the goodness of God alongside the goodness of all things He created. This is consistent with the first chapter of the Bible (this book cites the *New American Standard Bible*) where God pronounces the various stages of creation as "good" several times (Genesis 1:4, 10, 12, 18, 21, 25) before closing with the summation that all He created is "very good" (Genesis 1:31). The next step in Augustine's logical progression, the need to account for evil even though it could not have come from God, led to the foundation for mainstream Christian theodicy: evil is a privation. A privation is an absence of a goodness that ought to be present or a corruption of something that should be pure (Augustine, 1961:137-139, 148-150; Aquinas, 1989:18-20; Wright, 2006:113; Fernandes, 2002a:123-124; Hines, 2003:325; Geisler & Corduan, 2003:314, 329). God is all-good, and an all-good God ought not to be credited with the creation of evil.

However, since God created the earth, angels, and humanity *ex nihilo*, overly simplistic thinking could lead one to say that He must have created evil, whatever it is, even though it seems to be logically contradictory for an all-powerful and loving God to do so. The critical first step in this process is creation *ex nihilo*, and when carefully handled, the solution to the apparent problem presents itself. Since God created something out of nothing, then that something is part of His will and good plan; therefore, the fact of existence itself must be at least an order of goodness for that created thing (Augustine, 1961:148). Since the created things are finite and came from nothing, by nature they possess the possibility of a return to nothingness (nonexistence) as well as the possibility of decayed, diminished, or corrupted existence (Geisler, 2002:48; Boyd, 2003:63). If something good can either not exist or can exist in a corrupted form, then the *potential* for a lack of goodness exists—but the *potential for lack* is not an *actualized lack* of goodness itself. Only the actualized delta between the intended, maximum goodness of existence (the highest potential) and the degree to which it is actually good (the degree to which the highest potential goodness is realized) is evil. In this view the fundamental nature of created things allows for the possibility of corruption or nonexistence, and hence the possibility of evil (Geisler, 2002:46-48; Boyd, 2003:63).

Aquinas provides further clarity on this topic by recognizing that existence itself is not the ultimate measure of goodness. While existence is good, existence itself is only a *degree* of the potential goodness a thing can have, and the intended perfection of an object is dependent on attributes and abilities used to achieve the fulfillment of intended perfection (Aquinas, 1989:18-19). To give a concrete example, the lack of sight in a rock is not an evil since God did not intend for a rock to have the gift of sight; however, the lack of sight in a person would indeed be a privation. The concept of contextual privation makes it possible to claim that God did not create evil; He only created the possibility for evil to come into existence. The nature of all finite things is vulnerable to imperfection, and thus to privation and evil (Hines, 2003:325).

Moral Evil and the Fall

According to Genesis 3, Adam's disobedience to God in the Garden introduced evil into humanity. Adam could have resisted Satan's temptation, but he did not. For practical and experiential human purposes, the origin of earthly evil lies with the free-will choice of Adam to rebel against God and give in to the temptation placed before him (Schaeffer, 1968:81; Clendenin, 1988:326; Geisler, 2004:85-150). Choosing to do something either completely or partially deprived of moral rightness is evil, and the sin in the Garden was the first such human, moral privation.

Critics of Christian theodicy often point out that an all-powerful God could have created a world where people could not make the choice to do evil. However, the mainstream response of Christian theology is generally consistent. God is love, and He desired to create a world where true love was possible for its human inhabitants. This requires free choice as love must be voluntarily responsive and neither forced nor programmed (Geisler, 2002:58; 2004:231; Pinnock, 2001:126; Birch, 2003:146-147; Fernandes, 2002a:125-127; Moreland, 2003:66). In addition to that, the initial state of free will belonging to Adam is necessary for a moral world to exist. Morality requires freedom in order to be truly moral (Erickson, 1998:448-450; Geisler, 2002:58), and it must be truly free and not preconditioned, lest it not be true freedom (Bonhoeffer, 1997:16). True humanity requires freedom in order to actually be human, as opposed to something animalistic or robotic (Phillips, 1991:107).

Freedom itself is a good thing; however, it is the way one uses freedom that can lead to evil (Geisler, 2001:22-23; 2002:49; 2004:231; Moreland, 2003:66). The freedom to love God (or not to love Him) is an important part of the story of evil. Christianity claims that the deepest need of any human is the need for God, but genuine love requires that God not force anyone to respond in love to Him, lest it cease to be love. Thus the existence of evil becomes a possibility in a free, moral, loving world (Meilaender, 2006:126; Boyd, 2003:61). One should note that in no way is God responsible for the free choice Adam made. While He is responsible for the fact of freedom, He is not responsible for each individual's actualization of his or her own freedom. Thus, God is not the author of any human sin. He allows for the possibility of sin, but humanity is fully responsible for its sins (Althaus, 1966:156). "Let no one say when he is tempted, 'I am being tempted by God'; for God cannot be tempted by evil, and He Himself does not tempt anyone. But each one is tempted when he is carried away and enticed by his own lust" (James 1:13-14).

This is another point in which mainstream Christian theodicy makes a drastic departure from other theistic theodicies. The Bible teaches that Adam's sin caused him to descend into a corrupted state. This Fall became a devastating reality for all humanity as all people since that time are born into Adam's fallen state. They are inherently sinful, and they are unable to please God (Grudem, 1994:496-497; Erickson, 1998:656). The serpent (Satan) was already evil before Adam fell. Satan's rebellion and actions against God's will were evil as was his temptation of Eve. However, human sin was effectively the origin of evil in the world (pertaining to human existence) as it was Adam's sin, the Fall, that caused the curse. He could have resisted temptation and chosen not to sin, but he freely chose evil. It was the consequence of Adam's sin—not Satan's rebellion—that caused all people to be naturally sinful and to actualize evil (Fernandes, 2000:48; Erickson, 1998:452-455; Zacharias, 2000:136-137). Even Creation itself suffers from the evil that Adam's sin introduced (Romans 8:19-21). Some might claim that God sends evil upon people, but Fiddes concludes that even God's judgment is not evil itself, that in a case such as with Hosea's pronouncement of God's judgment, He is not inflicting evil upon the people; rather, they are being allowed to reap the natural consequences of their evil sin (1993:183). Taking the sinful nature of humanity a step further, Fernandes notes that the very establishment of human government itself is necessary to aid in protecting humanity from the self-inflicted evil because of the Fall (2003:19-20). In the Christian view, while the first instance of evil is Satan's rebellion, the Fall (original sin) and humankind's inability to please God are the origin of human evil and lead to its pervasiveness in the world and its impact on humanity. As already noted, this is not a view shared by Judaism, and the section on Islam will demonstrate that Islamic doctrine also does not hold to the doctrine of original sin.

The impact of the Fall is such that human attempts to conquer evil (to avoid any degree of privation) and to please God ultimately fail. Humankind's fallen nature is not something that human effort can overcome, and God, in His holiness and justice, will deal with evil in just fashion. Human efforts cannot overcome evil via good works that outweigh or cancel acts of evil (such as with the other theistic faiths included in this study), and only by God's acts will evil be overcome (Fernandes, 2002b:174-177). Human efforts produce no substantial, spiritual remedy as no one can please God or do good in His sight (Grudem, 1994:497-498). All human attempts at righteousness fall short, and some even argue that an attempt to fulfill the law (live in perfect righteousness) would be evil due to the immense self-pride necessary to believe one can achieve that lofty, godlike goal (Schreiner, 1999:219-220, 244).

The concept of holiness is a vital component of this discussion. People often define holiness as the complete and utter separation from evil. Holiness demands absolute perfection, not mere degrees of goodness that allow for inverse degrees of privation. Human goodness exists in degrees and therefore is not perfection itself (Zacharias, 2000:124). God alone is perfect, and therefore He alone is *completely* good. As Christian theology points out, God is immutable. The absolute perfection of God cannot change or degrade into degrees of goodness, which would allow for privation and evil (Aquinas, 1989:19-20; Augustine, 1993:381).

In addition, Otto's groundbreaking analysis of the Holy points out that the original concept of holiness in the scriptures denotes more than separation from evil; it communicates a sense that the Holy is something belonging to a different order than the human. It is a concept of something that is higher and greater than humanity. The Holy does not impart a sense of achievability on the creatures who apprehend it; rather, it imparts a sense of awe, wonder, fear, and creaturely dependence (Otto, 1958:5-11). Holiness is not achievable by human effort. The finite cannot bridge to the infinite; salvation from evil comes from God and not from the efforts of mere humans (Fernandes, 2002b:178). Humility, repentance, submission, and reliance on God are important to conquering evil (Augustine, 1993:708), and the only real goodness finite things of this world possess is found in the extent to which they point to and honor the Creator instead of elevating themselves (Bonhoeffer, 1997:26). In the end, it is all about God, His holiness, and His unique ability to save people from the evil they have wrought.

Concerning Natural and Physical Evils

Natural and physical evils can result in human suffering, and this is a vital part of the analysis of the Christian concept of evil. While much of the emphasis in Christian theology is on the metaphysical and moral nature of evil, one must not ignore the pain and suffering that is a part of every human's existence. Metaphysical and moral evils by themselves do not express the fullness of proper theodicy. The human experience of evil (perceived as undeserved pain and suffering) is a common, mainstream human aspect of evil. If one does not consider it, then one may argue that theodicy has favored disassociated intellect at the cost of human experience, and then it has largely failed in its purpose (van Inwagen, 1991:135; Williamson, 1983:44). In his moving account of the grief and suffering experienced as a result of his wife's death, C.S. Lewis points out that these instances of suffering are the occasions when

God seems least present and active. When an individual suffers, it feels as if God is not there (2001:5-6). The human experience of suffering is an important element that Christian theodicy must explain. The combination of several different views within Christianity seems to form a general Christian response to natural evils and human suffering.

One should note the finitude of human comprehension in a vast, complex existence. Suffering does occur, but sometimes giving a full answer for why or how a specific instance of suffering occurs may not be possible. This is a natural result of being a finite creature in a universe that is vast and complex, and only God can fully comprehend the myriad of interactions, reasons, and results. Therefore, seemingly arbitrary and inexplicable incidents of natural evil that lead to human suffering may well have good explanations, but the human mind may not be able to fully explain the interrelated elements that led to the suffering (Boyd, 2003:102-104, 152).

Keeping that in mind, one can argue that the world as it is today is not the best possible world that could exist. Just one less murder, rape, tsunami, disease, or starvation-inducing drought would increase the world by a commensurate degree of goodness. Many of the things that result from natural or physical evils are due to this not being the best possible world. Oftentimes the suffering experienced is a result of a specific moral evil such as a crime against a person (rape, torture, abuse). Some are unintentional consequences of one's own decisions, such as lung cancer that results after years of smoking or heart disease that results from overeating (Fernandes, 2002a:128), but other circumstances that cause suffering appear to be inexplicable and unexpected. Why, then, does God allow these evils to exist? Many Christians offer the theory that the best possible world may only be achievable through allowing people to make free, moral choices even if the consequences cause suffering; therefore, one must allow for the possibility and actuality of evil in order for the best world to develop (Geisler & Feinberg, 1987:334; Geisler, 2002:45).

This leads into a discussion about the will of God, specifically whether or not God deterministically wills that people should suffer. James 1:2 states, "consider it all joy, my brethren, when you encounter various trials." A simplistic interpretation would take this passage along with the promise of Romans 8:28 and assume that God wills specific instances of trials and suffering for the express purpose of developing certain attributes in believers. In response to this view, Isaacs delivers a powerful argument based on a grammatical analysis of James 1:2. Her conclusion is that the intention of James is to teach that one should neither view God as the source of trials, tests, and suffering that Christians are instructed to consider "all joy" nor blame Him for them (James 1:2; Isaacs, 2000:190-191). Biblical Christianity does not claim to offer easy, step-by-step solutions for the world's worst problems. The Christian life does not consist of simple answers that follow an easy, clear path; rather, it is a life that is complicated, confusing, and full of trials, tests, and even suffering (Allender, 2006).

Metaphysical Evil

The role of spiritual conflict in suffering is a vital part of Christianity's response to the problem of evil. Satan and the demons are constantly engaged in battle against God's will (Erickson, 1998:474-475; Grudem, 1994:420-423; Arnold, 1996:63-67, 75). Boyd points out that in the stories of Job and Daniel, spiritual conflicts played a role in those actual, physical circumstances, and that the victims were not (at least initially) aware of the spiritual aspect of the conflict. Job suffered as a result of a spiritual conflict of which he was largely ignorant, and the answer to Daniel's prayer was delayed due to a spiritual conflict with the "prince of the kingdom of Persia" (Daniel 10:10-21; Boyd, 2003:98, 103). With regard to the existence of evil, and especially with regard to human suffering, the role played by Satan and the demons looms large in Christian theodicy (Pinnock, 2001:134; Erickson, 1998:472-474; Henry, 1999:304; Flora, 1992:18-20; Clendenin, 1992:40).

Summary of Christianity's Concept of Evil

When considering the definition of the mainstream Christian view of evil for this comparative study, one must begin with an emphasis on the topic of privation. This concept is central to Christianity's theology, and it is significant when understanding its differences when compared to other theistic views of evil and suffering. In addition, one must take care to account for the role of human choice in actualizing evil out of potentiality. Finally, the concept of evil accounts for human suffering, just as it does with all religious traditions.

With the preceding points in mind, evil is defined as the privation of God's intended perfection for the goodness of creation, and in very simple terms it may be described as sin and suffering. It includes metaphysical and moral privations as well as the direct intended, direct unintended, and indirect, indecipherable, or chaotic consequences made manifest in the natural and physical experiences of human suffering. However, the widespread evil in the world originates and perpetuates in human rebellion against God, spiritual conflict (stemming from Satan's initial and ongoing rebellion), and the experiential consequences of a world at odds with God.

CHAPTER 4:

The Concept of Evil in Islam

Islamic Departure from Earlier Theistic Faiths

ISLAM HAS ITS ROOTS in the major, preceding theistic religions of the world with its ties to both Judaism and Christianity. To be more precise, in Surah 2 of the Quran (this study uses John Rodwell's English translation, see the bibliography for more details), it claims to be the same religion that God revealed to both the Jews and Christians previously. However, both of those groups forgot the pure truth, and their respective interpretations became perversions of the truth. This required the renewal of pure religion by way of a fresh, divine revelation. This revelation turned out to be the religion of Islam (Surah 2.81-87; Farah, 2003:86). Even though Islam claims to be a renewal of the truth revealed to both Judaism and Christianity, any study of Islam must begin by acknowledging the points of departure between the religions. These differences, many of which are polemic points of attack on the preceding faiths (Lazarus-Yafeh, 1996:62-64), vary in degree and scope; yet, they are key to understanding Islam's view of evil.

The first of the major differences is *tawhid*, the unity of God. While Christianity describes itself as monotheistic, Islam views the Christian doctrine of the Trinity as a violation of true monotheism. The divinity of Christ is particularly offensive in Islamic theology as it teaches that God has not ever been, nor will He ever become, incarnate. God is not human in any way. Because of that belief, the equation of Christ with God is *shirk*, which is the association of others with God (Miller, 2001:24; Farah, 2003:105, 108; Mohammad, 1985:383; Renard, 2002:200). The violation of the unity of God is the worst possible sin one can commit. It is an unpardonable sin, and one cannot mitigate the eternal consequences of this horrendous sin in any fashion. In the afterlife, those who commit *shirk* receive the worst eternal punishment. This serves to amplify the perceived severity of *shirk* (Surah 26.91-95; Farah, 2003:3, 117-118). While Christ is a non-divine sinless prophet, Islam views all prophets as sinless (Ali, 1990:175, 181). Christ's sinlessness does not equate to divinity, and he is neither divine nor the incarnate revelation of God as Christianity claims. This leads directly to the second major difference.

Islamic doctrine teaches that the Quran possesses the special quality of incarnate, divine revelation in somewhat similar fashion to the orthodox view of Christ in Christian thought. Islamic theology teaches that the Quran exists in the seventh level of heaven, and it pre-existed the creation of the earth (Arkoun, 2003:30; Farah, 2003:80). The heavenly Quran is the true Quran, it was written in Arabic (even in heaven), and the angel Gabriel's revelation to the Prophet Muhammad is the perfect revelation of the heavenly Quran (similar to the Word becoming incarnate). Muhammad did not author the Quran; he only recited what the angel gave to him directly (Martin, R., 1982:384). In Islamic theology, the Quran corresponds less to the Christian concept of scripture being inspired and inerrant and more to the Christian concept of *Logos* articulated in the first chapter of John. Thus, Islam claims to elevate the Quran nearly to the level that Christianity elevates Christ (Keddie, 1963:29-30; Mohammad, 1985:383). As Christ becomes the focal point for the Christian, so the Quran becomes the focal point for the Muslim. As such, the Quran is so holy that people must take extreme care in translation and distribution. This was demonstrated by the calls to execute two men who provided a translation of a copy of the Quran without including a copy of the original Arabic verses to prove they did not alter the Quran, and thus committed terrible heresy (Vogt, 2009). Despite the fact that the prophet received the revelation of the Quran nearly fifteen hundred years ago, it continues to provide timeless guidance for Muslims of all eras. As such, it is the ultimate source of truth, and it is the primary authority for the Islamic faith (Surah 2.1, 3.132; Mumisa, 2002:21; Gordon, 2003:90; Nettler, 1984:103; Farah, 2003:79; Renard, 2002:190). The Quran's historical importance at the edge of the Islamic frontiers in Morocco and Indonesia reinforce the concept of the strength and centrality of the Quran in Islamic culture. In these outlying areas, where other cultural and religious influences could have easily overwhelmed the new, local expressions of Islamic faith, Quranic scripturalism was the persistent, unifying force that helped preserve Muslim identity and Islamic consistency (Geertz, 1971:104-105). The pre-existence of the heavenly Quran mirrors certain aspects of Judaic tradition with regard to the Torah; however, the Quran possesses a greater degree of perfection and revelation than the Torah. As a result, while there is no intention of disparagement to the preceding theistic religions, Islam places a much greater emphasis on the importance of scripture and its full and perfect revelation. As Christ is the way of salvation in Christianity, the Quran is the perfect revelation from God that enables salvation for the Muslim. These two major departures from the other theistic religions form the base for moving forward in this study.

The Foundation for Evil in Islam

Evil is a strong and well-defined reality in Islam. As a result, Islam has developed a system of individual and societal rules to deal with evil.

As with the other theistic religions, anything contrary to the will of God is a proper starting place when determining the definition of evil. In Islam, God is the ultimate source of all good, and nothing good comes from any other source. Conversely, the general thought (echoed by all theistic faiths) is that nothing evil comes from God (Surah 4.81; Farah, 2003:7), although this general statement appears contradictory to some explicit doctrines (i.e., the evil impulse). In many ways, the foundational statements of mainstream Islamic theodicy imitate Augustine's musings on the nature of evil. However, while Islam has much in common with Christianity, it does not borrow the concept of evil as privation. With regard to this particular topic, it reflects a similarity to Judaism (and a similar theological conundrum as well) since it teaches that God created two specific things that influence people toward evil: Jinn and the bad impulse (Farah, 2003:113; Ali, 1990:142-144).

Jinn are the spiritual beings in Islam that are similar to angels in Judaism and Christianity, but Islam classifies them as lower than angels (Ali, 1990:128). Similar to angels, they are free-will creatures. God ordered Iblis (the closest equivalent of the Christian Satan) to worship Adam. Iblis refused to do so, and because of this, he is described as an "unbeliever" (Surah 2.32, 18.48, 20.15, 38.70-85; Nasr, 2003:64; Farah, 2003:113; Gordon, 2003:118). There is a subtle yet important piece of information to take note of in this designation of the disobedient Iblis as "unbelieving." The equivalence of belief and action is commonly expressed throughout the Quran (a limited set of examples includes Surah 5.12, 73; 13.28; 18.29, 87; 25.70; 29.6, 8; 31.21; 35.8; 40.60; 61.11-13; 64.9). The good deed does not naturally proceed from faith; the deed itself *is* the belief. This implies that there is no overriding sinful nature, since sins occur because of a lack of belief, not because of a corrupted nature, and several Islamic sources illustrate this point (Surah 2.34; Grunebaum, 1970:122; al Faruqi, 1973:198; Ali, 1990:178-181; Nasr, 2003:65).

The close relationship between belief and action leads to further differentiation in theodicy and soteriology. After the initial disbelief, Iblis and the Jinn acted as forces to encourage evil behavior (e.g., they were believed to be the ones to teach sorcery to Solomon). From this point on, Iblis is a personification of evil, and his destiny (along with the Jinn) is hell (Surah 2.96, 26.91-95; Nasr, 2003:64). The power ascribed to Iblis and the Jinn is less than that ascribed to the forces of evil in Christianity. Ultimately, Iblis and the Jinn encourage evil behavior in humans (Surah 2.163-164; Ali, 1990:139-143), and they are like the bad impulse in that they can influence people to sin.

Islam also teaches that God created two impulses that influence people, the good impulse and the bad impulse (Farah, 2003:113; Ali, 1990:143). According to the Islamic faith, people ought to overcome the bad impulse and live perfect lives (Sharif, 1959:42; Ali, 1990:175, 181, 193), while mainstream Judaism expects that people will sin several times during their life, even though perfection is a theoretical possibility (Steinberg, 1975:89; Heschel, 1976:393; Ariel, 1995:91). The Islamic doctrine of free will makes this expectation clear. Free will is a large, important part of Islamic theology, and many Islamic scholars still debate the concept of free will versus the constant Quranic theme of the divine decrees of God. However, careful analysis shows that there is ultimately no contradiction between the Quran's multitudinous mentions of God's divine decrees and its doctrine of humankind having free will. The seeming contradiction goes away if one notes that the concept of free will is limited to soteriological issues (Farah, 2003:119; Smith H., 1991:240-241). Therefore, Islamic sources reveal that humankind has free will when it truly matters (Asani, 2003:45; Farah, 2003:119; Smith H., 1991:240-241). Likewise, God does not decree in advance other less important actions of humankind with regard to committing evil or good acts; rather, they have their genesis in the will of the individual (Ali, 1990:235-241). God's *reactive* reinforcement of the authentic, free-will choice that an individual has already made reinforces the concept of the divine decree. The Quran shows this progression from free choice to downward spiral: "And whoso shall withdraw from the warning of the God of Mercy, we will chain a satan to him, and he shall be his fast companion for the satans will turn men aside from the Way, who yet shall deem themselves rightly guided" (Surah 43.35-36).

Consistent with the Islamic view of humankind's ability to fulfill the will of God perfectly, there is no original sin or fallen nature in Islam. When Adam made his mistake, the consequence was forgetfulness of truth, not a corruption of human will or the acquisition of a sinful nature. God then provided the people with revelation (an act of divine grace), and it is this revelation that re-enabled the forgetful people to perfectly fulfill His will, to fully resist evil, and to live without sin (Grunebaum, 1970:122; al Faruqi, 1973:198; Ali, 1990:157, 173, 178-181, 248; Farah, 2003:119-125; Nasr, 2002:8). This can also be discerned in the common, basic definition of Islam as complete surrender or submission to the will of God, and this submission ought to manifest itself in all of one's actions (Houben, 2003:149; Ali, 2008:12; Farah, 2003:3; Gordon, 2003:90). The strength of this conviction can be clearly seen as Nettler captures the Islamic view of the interplay of human and natural law with the claim that mankind's ability to perfectly fulfill the will of God is part of "God's immutable law of the universe" (1994:110). Individual perfection is possible in Islam for all believers and not just for the prophets, who are sinless (Sharif, 1959:42; Ali, 1990:157, 175, 181, 193; Nasr, 2003:46-47). In Islam, each individual must conquer the bad impulse, and it is in conquering the impulse that an individual develops toward his or her own perfection (Ali, 1990:144). Without decreed trials and suffering, and without the influence of the Jinn, humankind would have nothing to overcome and would be unable to develop toward perfection (Watt, 1979:18-19; Farah, 2003:123; Ali, 1990:144, 253-254). This again hints at a theology that merges faith with deeds, human law with natural law, religion with society, and God's revealed will with governmental operation and justice.

Free will and the individual's ability to fulfill the will of God lead to a key component of Islamic faith: the interrelatedness of belief and action. In at least thirteen Quranic passages, slight variations on the phrase "believe and do what is right" express an action-oriented directive relating to Islamic soteriology (Surah 5.12, 73; 13.28; 18.29, 87; 25.70; 29.6, 8; 31.21; 35.8; 40.60; 61.11-13; 64.9). In Islam, one's work is the same as one's faith—they are two sides of the same coin. Both faith and deeds are required for an individual's salvation as the deeds he or she performs during life largely determine one's fate in the afterlife (Surah 7.5-8, 10.27, 13.20-21, 23.1-10, 29.70; Farah, 2003:104-105; Nasr, 2002:246; Islam Online, 2001). At the final judgment, those who have not committed an unforgivable sin (such as violating the unity of God) will have their good deeds weighed against their evil deeds. Those whose good deeds outweigh their evil deeds receive good rewards and a place in paradise (Surah 39.70, 40.17, 41.46; Nasr, 2003:72-73; Ali, 1990:38, 210; Smith H., 1991:242). Those whose evil deeds outweigh their good deeds will receive evil rewards and hell (Surah 4.121, 17.7, 39.70). Residence in hell may be impermanent for those who do not commit *shirk* (more on this in a later chapter). Incorrect perceptions of God form the exception to this rule: if one's belief with regard to the unity of God is not correct (referring here strictly to intellectual acquiescence), then works will not count in one's favor, no matter their magnitude. That person will face eternal damnation along with those who neither believe nor work (Surah 3.20-21, 4.166-167, 10.28, 38.5, 39.25-27, 73). However, if one believes in the basic, Islamic-styled monotheistic doctrine of God without committing a heresy, even if one is not a Muslim proper, then one will have his or her works evaluated by God for soteriological purposes (Asani, 2003:44). To further emphasize that pure faith (without works) is not enough, the Quran specifically teaches that one who repents and has faith at the end of life will have his or her repentance rejected (Surah 4.22). In Islam both faith and deeds are necessary for salvation, which is the highest goal of the individual adherent.

The Unique Aspects of Islam's Concept of Evil

Evil manifests in the unwillingness (not inability) of an individual to conquer the bad impulse and in the choice to ignore the enabling divine revelation, and this leads to acts of evil. There is no sinful nature, and therefore everyone ought to be fundamentally good (Grunebaum, 1970:122; al Faruqi, 1973:198; Ali, 1990:178-181, 248; Nasr, 2003:65; Nasr, 2002:8). This basic concept is straightforward and bears similarities to the concept of evil found in Judaism. However, there are some unique aspects in the Islamic concept of evil.

By comparison with the other theistic faiths, some things labelled as evil are not immutable in their nature. As such, the nature of evil is subject to elimination or change, as with the circumstantial eating of pork (Mumisa, 2002:128) or the purification of evil in wealth (Nasr, 2003:95). While other theistic faiths share portions of this type of thought, it is carried significantly further in Islam. This thought pattern manifests in four major forms: the purification of evil, the cancellation of evil, the divine change of something from intrinsically evil to good, and the purging of evil through punishment (some aspects of these are detailed in the next few paragraphs).

One word for evil is *zulm*, which indicates something that is out of place or in deviation as opposed to it being intrinsically evil (Ali, 1990:237). Wealth is an example of something that is *zulm*, and Islam shows its unique approach to evil by using this concept. Paying the required tithe in obedience to one of the five pillars of Islam actually purifies an individual's wealth of *zulm*. This is not symbolic purification but is an act designed to nullify the *zulm* that is a natural, intrinsic, metaphysical part of wealth. In paying the tithe, one's entire wealth becomes purified, not just the portion that is given. While the concept of tithe is commonplace in theistic faiths, the thought of tithe as purifying something that would otherwise be evil is unique (Nasr, 2003:95). This introduces the subtle Islamic idea that much of what comprises evil is not absolute, but may instead be a function of time, place, context, and divine action. For example, God forbids individuals to eat pork (it is evil); yet one may eat pork if necessary for survival (Mumisa, 2002:128). In this example, the consumption of pork is not an evil that God forgives; rather, it is not evil at the outset due to the context of eating it. While Islamic theology initially labels many things as evil, there are conditions that change the actual, fundamental nature of the evil to good.

Sins in Islam are classified as major and minor, and the way they affect an individual changes dramatically, based on a variety of factors (*The Major Sins*, 2007; *What are the Major Sins?*, 2003). The minor sins count against an individual as evil, unless the individual is a serious Muslim and avoids the major sins. In that case, one of the following things can happen to the minor sins: they can be ignored by Allah; they can be fundamentally changed into goodness; they can be cancelled out by good deeds; or they can turn into a major sin if habitual (Farah, 2003:119; *Repentance for Major and Minor Sins*, 2003; *The Major Sins in Islam*:1). The lack of an immutable nature of evil (in most cases) leads to a perspective of evil and sin that allows for changes in the core nature of an individual's evil acts. The mainstream Islamic teaching that the performance of good deeds cancels out the evil deeds (Surah 5.15-16, 29.6, 61.11-13, 64.9; Ali 1990:344, 367) is relevant in terms of the mutability of evil. In other words, good deeds may render the evil deeds into a state of nonexistence. The context of the non-absolute nature of most evils provides a backdrop for another doctrine of mutability. Retroactive acts of God can change the minor evils committed by the faithful to goodness. This is different from contextually mutable evils such as eating pork. This doctrine concerns evils that are truly evil, but God changes their nature to goodness, and He will not hold those actions against a believer. "Those who shall repent and believe and do righteous works—for them *God will change their evil things into good things*" (Surah 25.70, emphasis added).

Finally, if none of the above occur or apply, a Muslim (this does not apply to heretics who have committed *shirk*) may be purged of sin by punishment. Some Muslims will go to hell, but for them hell is not permanent; it is a place of temporary punishment meant to purge their sin and bring them to perfection. They will enter paradise once their sin has been purged (Farah, 2003:118-119; Ali, 1990:226, 230-231). In this example, evil is not an attribute that is permanently applied to an individual in the afterlife; rather, evil can be an impermanent attribute. Once again, evil has a mutable nature for the Muslim believer.

Little about most evils is of a permanent nature for Islam. The purification, cancellation, changing, or purging of evil deeds is possible for most believers. There are, however, some major sins that will never be forgiven, such as major *shirk* (minor *shirk* would be insincerity or self-aggrandizement in religion). God will not forgive any person who does not believe or who violates the doctrine of His unity; their minor sins will remain minor sins; they will be held accountable and punished for all of them; their sins will never be purged; and he or she will suffer for all eternity. This includes apostasy, which is acting with ill will toward God, the Quran, or the Prophet (Surah 2.156, 3.8-10, 4.116-117, 10.28, 26.91-95, 38.5, 39.25-27, 73; Peters & De Vries, 1976-1977:10; Farah, 2003:3, 118). This exclusive soteriological system denies access to those who are sincere in the traditional, mainstream forms of all of the other major religions. This is not unique to Islam. All religions in their traditional, mainstream forms have fixed doctrines that preclude soteriological participation by those who follow the mainstream forms of other religions.

The Individual's Duty in Response to Evil in Islam

Islam teaches the ability and necessity of humankind to work to fulfill the will of God, the worth of good deeds in cancelling or changing evil for the individual, and the necessity of one to work toward individual salvation. Therefore, it is no surprise that among all theistic religions, Islam demands the greatest integration of religion with all aspects of life, including society and government. This plays a large role with regard to the concept of evil, and it affects how individuals must deal with evil in all aspects of their daily lives. Properly understood, Islam must encompass the *whole* of life. To be more specific, Islam demands a level of application that affects both one's life as well as the society in which one lives. In Islam, religion and politics should not be separated from one another, and a Muslim nation is supposed to be a force to conquer evil and spread good (including Islam) throughout the world (Moaddel, 2002:379; Moosa, 2000-2001:187; Houben, 2003:149; Mumisa, 2002:21). This movement toward Islamicization has led to common misunderstandings of two issues: fundamentalism and *jihad*.

Fundamentalism in its true form is the acceptance of and adherence to the fundamentals of Islam, which includes the struggle to integrate religion with society and government via peaceful methods (Nasr, 2002:108; Farah, 2003:404). So-called fundamentalists who are radical and violent in their acts may contribute to a misunderstanding of *jihad*, partly because of the role terrorism has played in recent history. The examples that may come to one's mind, such as the 9/11 attacks, are not consistent with the fundamentals of Islam or with the true doctrine of *jihad*, and the common Westerner often misunderstands these terrorist acts as reflecting the true, fundamental theology of Islam (Albertini, 2003:455-465; El Fadl, 2001:29, 33; Asani, 2003:46). With this in mind, most practicing Muslims follow the fundamentals, but because of the negative connotations associated with fundamentalism, they sometimes shy away from use of that label. However, a true Islamic fundamentalist will work toward peaceful integration with society and government (Nasr, 2002:108; Farah, 2003:404). This is where the more accurate definition of *jihad* plays a role in the life of the mainstream Islamic adherent: it is a struggle against personal and social evils, to right wrongs, to take personal responsibility for changing the world, and to spread Islam without compulsion (Nasr, 2003:97; Ali, 1990:407; Farah, 2003:413; Mohammad, 1985:385, 389). On the topic of spreading Islam without forcing people to convert, the Quran states it clearly, "Let there be no compulsion in religion" (Surah 2.257).

Approaching the Definition of Evil in Islam

Having laid the groundwork for the definition of evil by exploring Islam's theological foundation, one can formulate a broad definition of evil. It must allow accurate, cross-religion comparison on the theological, experiential, and philosophical considerations given to the issue of evil. Evil in Islam looks less like the concept of evil in Christianity and more like the concept of evil in Judaism. As such, the God-created bad impulse and the bad spiritual influences from the Jinn are where one can find some evil (Farah, 2003:113; Ali, 1990:119-144; Surah 2.163-164). However, its primary existence is in human decisions when they deviate from the will of God, since belief and action are so closely intertwined (Surah 5.12, 73; 13.28; 18.29, 87; 25.70; Farah, 2003:103; Ali, 1990:99-101, 104). There is no original sin and fallen nature (Surah 2.34; Grunebaum, 1970:122; al Faruqi, 1973:198; Ali, 1990:178-181; Nasr, 2003:65). When considering the definition from theological and philosophical perspectives, the bad impulse and the bad spiritual influences are not as important as some other elements because of Islam's theological explanation of the impulse and influences as being part of God's plan to lead humans toward perfection. Experientially, however, the challenges and suffering brought on by the impulse and influences are traditionally included in part of humankind's broad definition of evil; therefore, the definition of evil used for comparative purposes must include some amount of consideration for the human experience of evil and suffering.

The unique aspects of evil found in Islamic theology must also be given due consideration. Islam is the only major theistic religion that has a long, intricate process for discounting the existence and nature of evil in the lives of its adherents. Purification, cancellation, mutability, and purging can fundamentally alter evil for the Muslim believer. With this in mind, a definition of evil for Islam must be careful not to exclude its relative, personal mutability, while still maintaining overall precision of definition. This definition must include the doctrine of that which is the most opposite of evil (the greatest possible good). For Islam more than for any other religion, the definition of the greatest possible good includes actions as belief, and these actions extend to social and governmental considerations. *Qiyas* (human logic and reason), and *ijma* (the general consensus of Islamic society) aid one in understanding God's divine will and governing guidelines that are in the Quran, the *Shariah*, and the *Sunnah* (Mohammand, N, 1985:384; Metzger, 1994-1995:697-714; Mumisa, 2002:15). While its theistic counterparts in Judaism and Christianity show great concern for the well-being of people in general, Islam elevates and expands on this. The greatest possible good in Islam is when all individuals perfectly fulfill the will of God via their actions, since perfection is possible in Islam (Sharif, 1959:42; Ali, 1990:175, 181, 193), and this includes influence used to promote change in governmental and societal spheres (Moaddel, 2002:379; Moosa, 2000-2001:187; Houben, 2003:149). The opposite, therefore, is when people do not act in accordance with the revelation, and when societies do not function according to God's will.

The final component to receive specific mention is the doctrine of free will and the necessary, central role of human deeds as an intrinsic, inseparable part of proper faith. As the concept of human goodness is firmly established, the definition of evil must take care not to diminish the role of free will and the necessity of works in Islam.

Summary of Islam's Concept of Evil

With the overall goal of accurate comparison between major religions, with definitional consideration given to philosophy, theology, and human experience, and with the specific challenges and mandates unique to Islam, this study now presents the definition for evil in Islam. One can best describe the concept of evil in Islam as individual action, societal, and governmental function that is out of alignment (*zulm*) or in opposition to the will of God, and it also includes the human experience of trials and suffering of those who do not overcome as they should. Evil is generally an evil action or its consequences, and it can be eliminated or transmuted to a state of goodness except in extreme cases where the most basic of Islamic faith principles (Islamic monotheism) is denied.

Islam's unique approach to the problem of evil significantly distinguishes Islam from the preceding faiths. One might claim that Islam takes a few theological cues from Judaism (such as the two impulses) and then de-emphasizes and integrates those concepts with subtle, Eastern spiritual influences due to the mutability of evil deeds (which is something foreign to the other theistic systems but very familiar to karmic systems). More than any other religion, Islam's concept of evil emphasizes the necessity of humankind to work actively to change the entire world for the better.

CHAPTER 5:

The Concept of Evil in Hinduism

Defining Hinduism

THE CHALLENGE OF WORKING with a religion as varied and anomalous as Hinduism is immense. The breadth of spirituality in India lends itself to an amorphous religious experience that varies by region, tribe, and individual. One debated claim states that there is no real Hindu religion, and that Hinduism is simply a nineteenth century European word-construct that inappropriately attempts to create a universal whole out of tribal religions and philosophies that simply are not compatible with one another (Lorenzen, 1999:630). However, there have been many historical uses of variations of the word Hindu, and some of them reach as far back as Persian tablets dated from the sixth century BCE (Sharma, 2002:2). By the time of early Muslim interaction with the area now called India, the Muslims recognized a clear form of the Hindu religion and designated it as such (Sharma, 2002:5; Lorenzen, 1999:655). Even though European scholars may have lagged behind their near Eastern counterparts in recognizing it, Hinduism is a valid religious tradition with enough consistency to be recognized as such, and in modern times, it has taken its place among the world's great religions (van der Veer, 2002:175). All scholars who would seek to research Hinduism, both ancient and modern, must take a careful look at the variety of religious practices and philosophies that call themselves Hindu in order to determine which of the various beliefs practiced in that part of the world are universal and important enough to be part of the ultimate definition of mainstream Hinduism. Therefore, before proceeding with an analysis of the idea of evil in Hinduism, this study must lay the foundation for how to define mainstream Hinduism.

The Hindu Marriage Act of 1955 provided perhaps the broadest definition of Hinduism: anyone who lives in India and who does not claim devotion to a different, established religion is a Hindu (India, 1955). Even though the census bureau found that definition useful, the Second World Hindu Conference sought to narrow the definition further. They used the following criteria: anyone who prays, reads the Bhagavad Gita, worships a god, makes use of the mantra *Om*, and plants the *Tulsi* plant is a Hindu, although Michaels discounts the last point as specific to the particular sect of Hinduism that dominated the conference (Michaels, 2004:15). When considered with other sources, this definition does a fair job of narrowing the scope to something with a greater degree of precision than the definition offered by the Hindu Marriage Act of 1955. While this approach does aid one in finding a mainstream thread in the vast sea of Hindu practices, this definition is still weak. Its primary flaw is that it focuses on the specific actions performed by an adherent rather than making use of the underlying ideology for categorization and definition. Why, for example, is prayer and use of the mantra *Om* significant for a Hindu? For a Hindu it is clear, but for an outsider, this action-oriented approach to definition does not offer true clarity. Suppose, for example, that the definition of a Christian was written as "someone who attends a weekly meeting, ingests consecrated portions of bread and wine, prays, and who at some point has engaged in a modernized cosmogonic immersion ritual." As with the facetious definition of a Christian just offered, the definition of a Hindu offered at the Second World Hindu Conference does not contain sufficient meaning for a non-Hindu as it is presumed that the underlying doctrines and philosophies are self-evident. Therefore, while this definition accurately describes these actions as common Hindu activities, one must discern the underlying meaning before one can understand their significance.

Morgan offers a definition that addresses this deficiency by describing the most common beliefs that directly lead to the actions described earlier. First, Hindus accept the Vedas as sacred writings (scriptures). Second, Hindus believe that there is an ultimate ground of being that they call the Brahman. Third, Hindus believe that all people contain divinity within themselves (the Brahman). Fourth, Hindus believe that the doctrines of reincarnation and *karma* are true spiritual laws. Fifth, Hindus believe that all souls will eventually achieve liberation. Finally, Hindus believe that all religions lead to liberation *if they are correctly understood* (2001:12). When one analyzes this against the previous definition (actions), it is clearly different. However, the definition offered here by Morgan is actually the other side of the same coin (belief instead of action). The conference's use of prayer, the Bhagavad Gita, worship of *a* (not one, specific) god, and the use of the mantra all arise directly from the underlying Hindu concepts laid out in Morgan's definition, and it is from this point that this work shall continue. In particular, one should note the universality of Hindu beliefs regarding the Brahman and liberation. The two major themes that form the basis for Hindu thought are as follows: first, there is a single, ultimate reality, and the human soul is part of that reality. Second, that the highest goal of Hinduism is liberation from that which keeps one from intuitively knowing the truth about reality and the soul (Narayanan, 2003:129, 132, 156; Renard, 2002:257; Smith, H., 1991:22; Michaels, 2004:5; Ram-Prasad, 2001:379).

A further challenge in defining mainstream Hinduism comes from fringe Hinduism. Acceptance of the core beliefs (just listed) is what separates Hinduism from its distinct offshoots (such as Jainism and Buddhism); however, there is still a lot of contrast and variety to be found within the practices accepted as core, mainstream forms of Hindu religious expression. In Michaels' analysis of Hinduism, he perceived that most varieties of Hindu religious expression could fall under the mainline classification of Brahmanic-Sanskritic Hinduism. This well-developed approach accounts for the core, universal Hindu beliefs that manifest themselves in both urban and rural environments. It also accounts for the importance of the Vedas, the role of priests, the holy language of Sanskrit, and the multiplicity of paths to liberation. Finally, it is the dominant religious grouping throughout India, one that other non-Brahman groups attempt to join (Michaels, 2004:20). It is from this point of definition that this study of the Hindu concept of evil can begin.

Discovering the Idea of Evil in Hinduism

A survey of Hinduism reveals a problem that is difficult to resolve and requires careful study: Hinduism does not have a clearly defined sense of evil in the way that theistic religions do. The illusory or deceptive nature of perceived existence affects all aspects of Hindu thought, and it has a significant impact on their views of evil. Various Hindu scriptures communicate a little about evil, but they do not carry the explicit, theological weight one might expect. Hinduism generally appears to equate evil with undesirable personal behaviors rather than with an overarching moral concept or a foreboding spiritual foe. The challenge lies in discerning a mainstream system of evil that one can compare and discuss with the competing ideas found in other belief systems. In order to do this, one must pay careful attention to the implications and meanings of specific scriptural passages relative to the overall views of

Hinduism. For example, the Bhagavad Gita (3.36-43) teaches that desire drives people to evil. One can interpret this passage to imply that desire is evil due to its obfuscation of knowledge, and that knowledge possesses soteriological value. However, in this example, if one is to interpret both the explicit and implicit doctrines correctly, one must differentiate between the acquisition of general knowledge and the acquisition of knowledge that possesses soteriological, redemptive, or enlightening value. Obfuscation of general knowledge would not necessarily be an evil, and it is easy to misinterpret this particular passage and to forget the overall context. In another example, the Brihadaranyaka Upanishad (all Upanishads are listed in the bibliography under *Upanishads*) also speaks of evil, but it simply refers to it as something that "the Self is beyond" (IV:22).[1]

The Rig Veda presents one strikingly vehement use of the concept of evil. This particular passage describes several evil things: people who thrive on darkness, Brahman-haters, evildoers, people who plot evil, those who seduce a pure person, or deliberately change a person from good to bad (7.104.1-9). However, most of the items are not helpful when it comes to creating a definition of evil, as the words "darkness," "evil," and "bad" do not offer clarity as to what it is that actually earns those undesirable labels. In this context, these undesirable labels refer to a sorcerer—likely a rival priest—and this passage is in the middle of an incantation designed to wish evil and misfortune upon this rival. The vicious and vengeful nature of the passage does not serve to offer much in the way of a quality definition, even when attempting to define evil by contrast or antithesis. These problems are part of the challenges facing the definition of evil in Hinduism. What can be determined from the sources is that Hinduism does indeed have some concept of

1 Later in this chapter is an explanation of the differences between "self" and "Self"—the constant change between lowercase and capitalization is intentional when discussing Hinduism and Buddhism.

evil. However, it is clear that the Hindu concept of evil, much like the Hindu religion itself, is not going to be defined using explicit statements of propositional doctrine; rather, it will need to be extrapolated from the subtle patterns of negation and affirmation that make up the bulk of Hindu beliefs.

The next step is to determine what Hinduism defines as the greatest possible good, the ultimate goal, and the ideal acts of goodness. A basic survey of literature indicates some examples of what one might consider part of the ultimate good in Hinduism. These include liberation (Michaels, 2004:5; Ram-Prasad, 2001:379; Narayanan, 2003:156), singular existence (Renard, 2002:257), the immortality of the soul (Narayanan, 2003:132), or to move beyond imperfection (Smith H., 1991:22). It logically follows that whatever is the most antithetical to these things can be considered evil. That which is the nearest opposite of the greatest good is the greatest bad. Whatever prevents one from achieving the ultimate goal is part of what constitutes evil, and the human actions that counteract or prevent things defined as good actions are included in the definition of evil.

An analysis of Hindu writings reveals support for this pattern. Many of these writings express the rich tradition of teaching by way of contrast and negation. "*Neti, neti*" is a commonly known phrase that means "not this, not this." Its purpose is to define and teach by way of negation and antithesis (Rao, 1970; Chaudhuri, 1954:44). One must be careful, however, not to misapply this technique by applying it in the wrong situations. This is a religious tradition that often deals with seemingly antithetical concepts that in the end turn out to be aspects of a unified whole. Rudra (a probable forerunner to Siva), for example, is a god described in the Rig Veda who is praised as the source of healing and mercy, but in seeming contradiction, Rudra is also a deity that is feared as something that kills and destroys (2.33.1-14). One must take care to use proper contextual identification before application of negation in order to avoid inappropriate and misleading use of this technique. Nonetheless, this overall approach plays a large role in Hindu scriptures themselves, as many of the scriptures make use of this method throughout (the Brihadaranyaka, Katha, Isha, and Tejobindu Upanishads, as well as the Bhagavad Gita). Therefore, this study will carefully apply this technique, which is consistent with Hindu methodology.

Identification of Foundational Hindu Concepts

There has been some debate as to whether or not Hinduism is pantheistic or monotheistic. Hinduism teaches that there is only one, singular, ultimate reality, which is God *and* the universe together as one: "I permeate all the universe in my unmanifest form. All beings exist within me" (Bhagavad Gita 9.4). Since the apparent plurality of Hindu gods is ultimately viewed as individual aspects or manifestations of the one, singular, ultimate reality or God (Morgan, 2001:71; Smith H., 1991:36, 62; Smith F., 2000:256-257), one may be tempted to label Hinduism as monotheistic. However, the definition of monotheism specifies the existence of only one God, who is *distinct and separate from the universe* (van Baaren, 2008; Wainwright, 2005). One could argue for the application of some other labels, such as pantheistic, polytheistic, monistic, or henotheistic, with some degree of success. Nevertheless, application of the monotheistic label is not a valid conclusion (Walston, 2007); rather, it is a move toward inappropriate religious syncretism.

Yet this concept of the singular, ultimate reality is the foundation of all Hindu thought. Named the "Brahman," the importance of this concept can be discerned in widespread writings where it is described as the Immortal, The All, God, the universe, all mind, all matter, truth itself, and unity without duality (Bhagavad Gita 11.7; Brihadaranyaka Upanishad IV:32; Mandukya Upanishad I:2; Isha Upanishad I:17; Rao, 1970:378-380). Hinduism also claims that individual existences (Self/self) are not ultimately distinct from the Brahman, and that all distinction is ultimately delusory. For ongoing reference in this study, when Hindu scriptures are translated into English, both the true Self (nonphysical) and the illusory self (physical) are translated into the same, basic English word, "self," but they are differentiated by capitalization of Self (Atman, true self, nonphysical) and the non-capitalization of self (non-Atman, illusory self, physical). This study will use the same approach throughout the sections that focus on Hinduism.

The "Atman" is the true Self (or soul) within each individual while the non-Atman is the illusory portion of existence that people incorrectly perceive as self. The true Self is identical to the Brahman (Morgan, 2001:63-65; Smith, H., 1991: 21, 30, 67; Chaudhuri, 1954:52). Two portions of scripture bring this to an explicit point: "The Self is indeed the Brahman" (Bridaharanyaka Upanishad IV:5), and "Brahman is all, and the Self is Brahman" (Mandukya Upanishad I:2).

As all states of being proceed from the unity of the Brahman, it follows that there is one underlying law that governs existence, truth, and human behavior. This is indeed the case, and Hindus call this "dharma." The Hindu concept of dharma (which varies slightly from the Buddhist concept) contains the basic existential laws of how the universe functions, including the mandated realities of a merely illusory self-existence such as birth, death, creation, and destruction (Michaels, 2004:15-16; Creel, 1972:155-156; Shulman, 1979:669). Dharma also goes beyond the laws governing basic existence. It includes concepts of religious duty and human behavior. Of particular note is that there is personal dharma that is relative to each individual. Each person should behave according to his or her current state, which is unique to each individual. In this regard, dharma can mean the way one ought to act, similar to the concept of a correct path for life (Michaels, 2004:15-16; Creel, 1972:155). A fifteenth-century poem uses dharma to refer to any set religious path when it refers to the ways of the Hindus and Muslims (Lorenzen, 1999:651-652). For a non-Hindu, particularly for a monotheist who believes in the distinction between God and the universe, the use of dharma that simultaneously refers to universal laws of existence, proper societal religious behavior, and personal actions may appear to be an inappropriate grouping of disparate topics under a single label. However, it is important to keep in mind that Hindu thought does not differentiate between religious behavior, social behavior, the laws that hold the universe together, the reality of death and destruction, and the reality of God, who *is* the universe (Michaels, 2004:15-16; Shulman, 1979:669; Creel, 1972:155-156). It is all the same thing; therefore, the concept of dharma as truth, law, and the personal, proper way is internally consistent. To narrow it to a single aspect would be inaccurate. Having the concept of dharma allows for discourse on what constitutes evil (anti-dharma) actions. One must understand why Hinduism defines dharma as it does in order to interpret the underlying religious philosophies accurately. This leads to a clarified understanding of evil in the Hindu system.

The Hindu concept of *maya* provides important insight into the nature of self and the world. Maya is the illusion of multiplicity that prevents one from perceiving true, unitive existence with the Brahman. It is the physical "reality" people experience. The concept of maya leads to the belief in a material existence that people *perceive* as real, but it is actually a veil of delusion that covers true existence. One may even say that perception itself is mistake or delusion (Roach & McNally, 2005:8). It may help to explain this as the difference between mind (Self/Brahman) and matter (self/maya). If one does not see through this veil and identify oneself as part of the Brahman, one will incorrectly believe that maya is true existence and never realize the truth. Even God or the gods are maya in that they are limited, imperfect manifestations of the Brahman (Michaels, 2004:209, 263; Morgan, 2001:37).

Identifying Evil in Hinduism

All Hindu doctrines point the faithful toward liberation, although the methods employed to reach that goal will vary greatly—even to the point of seemingly having a different goal. However, the underlying goal remains consistent regardless of the varying expressions of faith. Careful interaction with Hindu sources reveals that liberation is the move beyond self and the veil that covers true existence in order to achieve a unitive state (when the self realizes the unity between Self and Brahman). In achieving *moksha*, or liberation, the Self realizes its intrinsic immortality (identification as Brahman), and the fullness of *true being* is realized. All Hindu paths to moksha lead an adherent to a direct experience of Atman-Brahman. When this happens, the Self, no longer crippled by the self, realizes the pure being, consciousness, and bliss of Brahmanic unity. Liberation also frees one from *samsara* (the cycle of death and rebirth) and the responsibility of individual dharma (Narayanan, 2003:129, 156; Renard, 2002:257; Ram-Prasad, 2001:379, 387; Michaels, 2004:5, 157; Morgan, 2001:36, 53; Smith, H., 1991:21, 60; Creel, 1972:163-165; Rao, 1970:378-380; Chaudhuri, 1954:49). Lest anyone doubt the core theological position of non-duality (the true, unitive nature of existence), liberation is clearly described in the Katha Upanishad: "As pure water poured into pure water *becomes the very same*, so does the Self of the illuminated man or woman, Nachiketa, *verily become one with the Godhead*" (part II, I:15; emphasis added).

Liberation is the ultimate goal of Hinduism, thus it follows, both logically and by Hindu tradition, that the concept of evil is that which is conceptually nearest the opposite of the Atman-Brahman unitive state. It also includes those things that prevent unity and liberation. The Kena Upanishad, for example, states that "those who realize Brahman shall *conquer all evil* and attain the supreme state" (III:9; emphasis added). If the Self-realization of Brahman conquers evil, then those things that fight against liberation and reinforce the veil of maya and the illusion of selfhood are the Hindu realities of evil. Hinduism describes many things as actively working against the ultimate good of unity with the Brahman. These include violence, deceit, theft, impure sexuality, greed, passions, hatred, ego-centrism, attachment, ignorance, selfishness, physical pain, unmet desires, restricted being, belief in duality, acceptance of human finitude, and even the desire to continue living (Morgan, 2001:42-43, 67; Smith, H., 1991:21-24; Renard, 2002:257, 264; Tejobindu Upanishad; Bhagavad Gita 2.62-67, 3.40-41, 16.3-17). An analysis of these hindrances to liberation reveals a pattern (similar to what will be seen in Buddhism): they all have the end effect of causing one to believe in, value, and act for self instead of Self. As such, the acts themselves are evil because they perpetuate an intrinsically harmful delusion of duality that prevents the ultimate good. These evil acts also accumulate negative *karma* for the doer.

Some have described karma as Hinduism's theodicy. It is Hinduism's explanation for why humans live in delusion and reap their due share of negative consequences (Michaels, 2004:156). When one looks closely at the idea of karma, one can see that Hinduism posits the universe as a purely just place. How else could it be when it is all Brahman? Everything an individual self experiences is a direct result of actions, deeds, and perceptions accumulated during current and previous incarnations that are still present at the death of one's previous self. In this view of the universe, the conclusion is that nothing happens by chance; a person directly earns everything that affects him or her in life. If negative karma burdens the self at the time of death, then the Self must take on a new self through as many incarnations as are necessary to purge itself of karma. Only after the expiation of karma is the incarnate self able to intuitively and experientially realize the true Self and achieve liberation (Brihadaranyaka Upanishad IV:5; Shvetashvatara Upanishad V:11; Good, 2000:281; Narayanan, 2003:156; Creel, 1972:161;

Shulman, 1979:652). While the rewards and punishments of karma must be experienced, karma itself is not evil; it is the balancing nature of the universe, part and parcel of the reality of dharma. Accordingly, the apparent lack of justice in human existence is nothing more than one's lack of proper perspective. All is working karmically as it should be (Morgan, 2001:34). When the mortal Arjuna expresses discomfort at the thought of killing worthy men in battle (and thereby creating widows and orphans), Krishna explains to him that there really is no unjust killing, as killing a self is killing something that is fundamentally illusory. Krishna asks Arjuna, "Knowing that it [the Self] is eternal, unborn, beyond destruction, how could you ever kill? And whom could you kill, Arjuna?" (Bhagavad Gita 2.21). Later in the conversation, he exhorts Arjuna to perform "all actions for my sake, desireless, absorbed in the Self, indifferent to 'I' and 'mine,' let go of your grief, and fight" (Bhagavad Gita, 3.30). Preconditioned delusion causes one's perception of injustice or evil in undesirable circumstances, such as those containing death and destruction, to be flawed. In fact, the recognition of destructive forces as divine (and therefore good) is a common aspect of Hinduism (Shulman, 1979:668). Krishna illustrates this when he speaks with pride: "I am death, shatterer of worlds, annihilating all things" (Bhagavad Gita 11.32).

Summary of the Concept of Evil in Hinduism

One can delineate a definition of evil in Hinduism after carefully analyzing the preceding beliefs. Evil deeds are those deeds that accumulate negative karma, work against dharma, proper perspective, and the unitive state. Likewise, thoughts, ideas, and philosophies that lead toward self, duality, and embracing maya are evil. Two sections from the Katha Upanishad sum this up well: "The Self cannot be known by anyone who desists not from unrighteous ways, controls not his senses, stills not his mind, and practices not meditation" (II:24). These hindrances to good described here are unrighteous ways (actions), uncontrolled senses (perceptions), un-stilled minds (desires), and the lack of meditation (direct experience of truth of the Brahman). All of these things work to enforce the perception of self, duality, and maya. The Katha Upanishad goes on to list the consequences. It is a point of great emphasis as the following line is repeated two times in the space of four sentences: "Who sees multiplicity but not the one indivisible Self must wander on and on from death to death" (part II, I:11).

Hinduism is a religion of plurality and variation. Nevertheless, it contains enough consistency for one to define it as a mainstream religious tradition, and it possesses a concept of evil that is unique. The foundational beliefs of Hinduism are monistic, and as such, the Hindu faith teaches its adherents to reject duality and seek unity with the ultimate reality. Unlike monotheistic religions, Hinduism does not explicitly delineate the concept of evil, but one can discover its equivalent concept by analyzing the core components of faith and goodness and by determining their most antithetical concepts and harmful behaviors. As the goal of Hinduism is liberation from duality and unity with Brahman, the definition of evil contains those things that reinforce the concepts of duality and the individual self along with those things that prevent realization of the unitive state.

Non-duality remains at the heart of Hindu beliefs. Any deviance toward dualism (even in the well-known path of individual devotion) is unacceptable, and one may describe it as evil.

CHAPTER 6:

The Concept of Evil in Buddhism

Preliminary Thoughts on Evil in Buddhism

FROM ITS INCEPTION IN India approximately 2,500 years ago, Buddhism has quickly risen to become one of the world's great religions. As with Hinduism, Buddhism has no absolute God in the way that theistic faiths do, and concepts of sin and morality are murky by comparison. Therefore, defining evil in Buddhism is a challenge (much as it is in Hinduism). There is no clearly defined concept of evil one can grasp onto as a starting point. However, the absence of a clearly labeled evil does not mean that there is no equivalent concept. In fact, Buddhism has an extensive tradition of examining the philosophical issues surrounding Buddhist equivalents of evil as well as the human experience of suffering. In addition, Buddhist teachers exhort their followers to do no evil in the course of their lives (Davis, 1989:312; Fox, 1971:35-36).

When it comes to discovering the broad definition of evil in mainstream Buddhism, this study will use the same approach that it used with Hinduism since many of the challenges are similar. One can discern Buddhism's sense of evil by discovering that which is the most philosophically opposite or incompatible with Buddhist philosophy's concept of good. In experiential terms, it is that which causes, or is the source of, or reinforces the opposite of the greatest possible good.

At this point, it is valuable to provide a brief historical context for this analysis. Buddhism sprang out of Eastern and Hindu thought around 500 BCE. However, while it shares a common root with Eastern thought, a common worldview (pantheism), and some similar concepts (dharma and karma), one should be careful not to consider Hinduism and Buddhism as homogenous religious traditions. In the Hindu perspective, Siddhartha Gautama (the Buddha) is a heretic (Morgan, 2001:99). Siddhartha Gautama was a Hindu prince who decided to seek truth and inner peace. He rejected many Hindu teachings and achieved enlightenment on his own after deviating from the common Hindu paths for seeking enlightenment. The Buddhist doctrines the world knows today are a result of his enlightenment. In short, by rejecting the supposedly cruel and indifferent views of Hinduism, which taught that suffering is more illusory than real, he taught that the suffering perceived by humans is indeed real. He also taught that suffering could end. In addition to making these claims, he also presented the way by which individuals can cease their own suffering. Buddhist adherents view Siddhartha Gautama as having discovered a better way in the Hindu world—one that they claim is far less cruel than Hinduism since Siddhartha Gautama's approach acknowledges suffering—and they gave him the title of "the Buddha," which means the "Enlightened One" or the "Awakened One" (Smith, H., 1991:82). Despite similarities between the two faiths, Buddhist and Hindu beliefs are distinct. As one can learn from one analysis of Dharmapala's actions at Bodhgaya, Hindu attempts to fit the Buddha and his enlightenment within a Hindu perspective have often clashed with the Buddhist desire to differentiate and separate itself from Hinduism in order to avoid assimilation and dilution of its own distinct, specific views (Kinnard, 1988:817-839).

Varieties of Buddhism

As with many religions, Buddhism has several different sects and practices. However, the major differences between the schools of thought are not generally as critical or divisive as the doctrinal differences between the different denominations in theistic religions. For the purposes of this study, the differences between the various mainstream expressions of Buddhism do not have a significant impact on the overall Buddhist view of the concept of evil. Nonetheless, one should be aware of a couple of major distinctions between Buddhist systems. The first distinction is whether enlightenment is for individual people only or if enlightenment is meant to be, and indeed eventually *must* be, achieved by all people. The second distinction is in the minimum length of time it takes to achieve enlightenment. Theravada Buddhism is the form that is most common in southern Asia, and it emphasizes personal enlightenment via non-harming, personal purification, simplicity, and moral living (Das, 1998:62-63). Mahayana Buddhism is the dominant form of Buddhism in eastern Asia, including China, Japan, and Korea. Mahayana Buddhism has also exerted great influence on other Buddhist traditions such as the Tibetan schools. It emphasizes a wide interdependence between all things and a concern for collective humanity as opposed to individual spiritual excellence. Analysis of Mahayana writings and the Bodhisattva Vow shows a need to work for the good of all and for universal enlightenment (Hershock, 2003:253; Cohen, R. 2000:30; Makransky, 2000:54-58; Das, 1998:143). Perhaps best known outside of Asia in Europe and the Americas is Tibetan Buddhism. As arguably the most recognizable leader in Tibetan Buddhist traditions, the Dalai Lama leads a branch of Buddhism that expresses a more mystical side of the Mahayana tradition, and his mission to spread loving-kindness and compassion throughout the world has brought both him and his religion much attention the world over. Still other traditions, such as Zen Buddhism from Japan, emphasize the ability of an individual to attain sudden, instantaneous enlightenment by breaking through and bypassing normal, human thought patterns. In this system, an individual can experience *satori* (instantaneous enlightenment) and can achieve enlightenment during one's first lifetime (Gethin, 1998:262).

While there are many varieties of Buddhism, the differences do not present difficultly in this study of evil since all Buddhists pursue the same thing (enlightenment) as guided by the same general form of thought (though some particulars change). It is this individual pursuit of enlightenment, which can be described as the individual's fight against "evil," that is of note in the context of this study. While it is important to acknowledge a wide variety in practices and particulars, Buddhist thought concerning evil is generally consistent throughout its various expressions.

Buddhist Acknowledgment of the Existence of Evil as Demonstrated by Suffering

Buddhism specifically acknowledges the true, actual, experiential existence of suffering as demonstrated by the First Noble Truth taught by the Buddha. It is from this point that one can begin to construct the concept of evil in Buddhism. The importance of the First Noble Truth should not be understated. While people asked the Buddha about a wide variety of metaphysical speculations, he claimed to teach only one theme: the existence and extinguishment of suffering (Das, 1998:190). Dharma and karma are key parts of this teaching.

Dharma emerges as the Buddhist idea that blurs the concepts of philosophical truth, ethical actions, and reality itself. One should not consider the dharma solely as a way to act or simply as a concept. It is *the* way for one to act, as well as *the* philosophical approach to knowledge, as well as *inescapable reality itself* (Gethin, 1998:35). Implicit within the dharma is the law of karma as well as all the Buddhist concepts about reality and suffering. In fact, a Buddhist may not even call the dharma a human view of reality, but perhaps he or she would more accurately call it reality revealed. Since dharma is reality, and since one of the fundamental human problems according to Buddhism is ignorance of the true reality, Buddhists then seek to live the dharma. Suffering arises when people fail to do this, and then circumstances born out of negative karma plague them. The law of karma states that there are rewards and penalties for everything that an individual does. Some deeds are more in line with dharma and some are at odds with it. Bad deeds carry over in this life (and the next) and bring suffering, while good deeds gain positive karma (which expiates the bad karma) and lead to rewards, happiness, and enlightenment (Eckel, 2003:185). Common phrases such as "you reap what you sow," "do unto others," and "what goes around comes around" are common expressions of this type of thought. The law of karma also teaches that the very existence in which one currently lives, the circumstances and conditions of an individual's life—including suffering—are a direct result of his or her own personal karma.

Suffering, in the Buddhist view, does not refer to just physical affliction or mental torment. While it can be those things, it can also be much subtler. The term for this suffering is *dukkha*. A careful analysis of Buddhist writings shows that the connotations commonly associated with the English word "suffering" are not nuanced enough for casual observers (Fonner, 1993:5; Smart, 1984:371-372; Gethin, 1998:61). Fonner describes three specific types of dukkha in his explanation for why the use of the word "suffering" is inadequate. He acknowledges that physical suffering is the first definition of dukkha, but then in his second and third definitions he describes dukkha as generally pertaining to mental, emotional, or spiritual conditions. He uses descriptions such as unsatisfactoriness, dis-ease, disenchantment, and disillusionment for these alternate definitions (1993:5). However, while Fonner stresses the need to avoid using the word "suffering" too broadly, one can categorize all of his alternative descriptions under the broad use of the word. As the proposed alternatives fall into a common-sense understanding of suffering (and as the vast majority of Buddhist writings that have been translated into English make extensive use of the word "suffering"), use of this term is proper in the Buddhist context.

In mainstream Buddhist thought, suffering is the primary and universal affliction of human life, and as such, it is highly undesirable. Therefore, the cessation of suffering—via enlightenment—is the ultimate goal of the Buddhist adherent regardless of which particular school of Buddhism the individual practices (Burton, 2002:326; Gethin, 1998:59). When attempting to apply the concept of evil to Buddhism, one must focus on the opposite of the highest goal or on that which prevents people from reaching the goal. As suffering prevents people from reaching enlightenment, it naturally follows that suffering is equivalent to the greatest evil. In support of this, one can read Buddhist sources and discern that one key approach to defining good and evil is to measure the suffering one eliminates or causes in life (Goleman, 2003:76).

As evil (i.e., suffering) does exist in Buddhism, one must examine its pervasiveness in human existence and experience in order to get a sense of the scope and importance of the topic. In the *Majjhima-nikāya* (a portion of the Buddhist canon of scriptures), the extent of human suffering can be seen to be great indeed. Birth, aging, sickness, death, sorrow, pain, desire, and many more things are sources and experiences of human suffering. After considering this, one may assume that all of life or existence itself is suffering. Careful engagement with the sources shows that this is an inaccurate conclusion. Rather, although this portion of scripture acknowledges that suffering (evil) is pervasive in human existence, not everything about life is suffering. However, life by its very nature is difficult and flawed (Das, 1998:77).

While life itself is not suffering, dukkha underlies all human existence. This concept blurs the line between suffering *as life* and suffering as an *attribute of life*. It means that something about life is not right, that something is off-balance, and that this way of experiencing existence is universal (Ryan, 2003:144). The Buddhist concept of dukkha expresses that suffering noticeably taints all life, and humanity in general has a sense that things are not as they should be. Sometimes it takes the form of physical suffering, but it can be emotional or mental suffering as well. With this in mind, according to the Buddhist belief system, evil as related to suffering is real, pervasive, and damaging.

The Cause of Suffering in Buddhism

However, the actuality and importance of suffering does not complete the concept of evil. One must also consider the source of suffering. If there is a right way for an individual to live, a way that decreases suffering, then that is "good." Contrariwise, if there is a wrong way of living that increases suffering, or if there is a metaphysical source of suffering, it is "evil."

The Second Noble Truth of Buddhism demonstrates that suffering has a cause. Craving emerges as the key when one examines Buddhism for the source of suffering (Ryan, 2003:144). The word "craving" carries a connotation that is undesirable (perhaps akin to envy or jealousy). To claim that all craving is undesirable may appear unnecessarily extreme to non-Buddhists. However, in order for one to understand the Buddhist position, it is not possible to examine the source of evil and suffering (as craving) without first examining the underlying worldview. This brings everything into focus and explains just how critical the concept of craving is.

The first item one must understand is that the concept of self as Westerners understand it is incorrect. Also, while the Buddhist view of self is more similar to the Hindu view than to the theistic view, one should also take care to note that it is notably different from the Hindu definitions of self and Self. Buddhist sources show that the self is nothing more than an aggregate of various changing perceptions and moments.

Goleman recorded Matthieu Ricard explaining this to the scientists at Mind and Life VIII with eloquence:

> There is a very deep approach in Buddhist philosophy and practice to try to examine if that 'I' is just an illusion, just a name we attach to that stream and flux in continuous transformation. We cannot find the 'I' in any part of the body, or as something that would pervade the body in its entirety. We might think that it lies in the consciousness. But consciousness is also a stream in continuous transformation. The past thought is gone, the future one has not yet arisen. How can the present 'I' truly exist, hanging between something that has passed and something else that has yet to arise? And if the self cannot be identified in the mind or the body, nor in both together, nor as something distinct from them, it is evident that there is nothing we can point to that can justify our having such a strong feeling of 'I.' It is just a name one gives to a continuum (Goleman, 2003:79).

In core Buddhist teachings, the various items that make up the human *sense* of self (not actuality) are described as a mixture of perception, feeling, changing dispositions, intelligence, and form (Chen, 2001:26; Radhakrishnan & Moore, 1957:272; Das, 1998:118). This doctrine of "no self" teaches that there is no core personhood or governing entity contained within what an individual perceives as oneself (Das, 1998:119). In other words, the sense of identity that people think they really experience is actually a delusion. Any idea that there is something more than the momentary aggregate of the five *skandhas* (form, feelings, perceptions, intentionality, and consciousness) to human existence is incorrect, misleading, and ultimately harmful. However, one should not be quick to label this as a doctrine of nihilism. To teach nonexistence is heretical—just as the teaching of actual existence is heretical. Buddhism expounds on the "middle way" between nonexistence and the actuality of self. The Buddhist texts generally agree that the sense of self that people experience arises from the continuum of the five senses (Gethin, 1998:78; Goleman, 2003:79).

If the self does not exist, then all craving to satisfy some perceived need of the self is intrinsically delusory, and it serves only to perpetuate the delusion. This is the point at which craving enters the analysis of evil. If existence is truly a stream of changing processes and experiences, then the world as it is perceived by humans must be constantly changing or have a dreamlike quality of existence (Das, 1998:329). In support of the argument for the changing nature of existence, it is logical to point out that the very nature of happiness, pleasure, and joy imply the very lack of the same. How does one know what joy is if not for a lack of joy? If pleasure is intrinsic to, unchanging in, and not lacking in one's own existence, then one would not be able to distinguish it as pleasure and be able to say, "I am happy." That person could only say, "I am." To claim an attribute of existence is to acknowledge the possible lack of that attribute or at least the existence of an opposing attribute.

In Buddhist philosophy, the attributes and circumstances of human existence change. Some of the things a person possesses (such as happiness) will go away or diminish. The laws of cause and effect change everything about life; everything is in a constant state of change (Das, 1998:118). The thought continues on to say that because these attributes of perceived existence change, people will experience pain. That which one grows accustomed to and desires will not always be available, and because of this, an individual will experience pain or suffering because of the change. He or she will then develop aversions to those things perceived to cause suffering (Burton, 2002:326). Aversion is reversed craving (craving the absence of something), and it perpetuates the delusion of a core self. Craving is a downward spiral that gains in momentum and leads to further pain and delusion—one that death does not end.

In Buddhism, death is not the gateway to eternity. After all, there is no self that dies. This is where evil (as craving) perpetuates into the next lifetime. Unless one eliminates the chain of craving and suffering, this connected pattern of the five aggregates, which is mistaken for a self, will continue by way of reincarnation (Bond, 1980:240-241). The cravings and aversions developed as part of the delusion of self persist into subsequent incarnations unless one purges them. *Samsara*, the cycle of death and rebirth until enlightenment is achieved, is evident throughout Buddhist writings, and an individual's participation in samsara is indicative of that person's need to purge craving and accept (literal) selflessness or a doctrine of emptiness (Keenan, 2002:142; Dillon, 2000:538; Rupp, 1971:55-67). One should not view the Buddha as someone who offered a way to avoid death or illness. Instead, he taught that one needs only to curb desire by rectifying one's own existential view to the truth of no self, personal emptiness, or Buddha-nature (Cho, 2002:433-434; Seiichi, 2001:95-99; Fox, 1971:36-38). Regardless of differences between Buddhist traditions with regard to some of the particulars, the core of belief with regard to suffering remains the same: the denial of self and the cessation of craving.

Summary of Buddhism's Concept of Evil

Buddhism has a significantly different concept of evil than theistic religions. Still, the concept of evil pervades Buddhist thought. Evil is suffering, ignorance, and craving. This is the underlying foundation of the First and Second Noble truths. While similar to the Hindu concept of evil, there are important differences, in particular the all-important role of suffering in Buddhism as exemplified by the First Noble Truth. While there are many expressions of Buddhism that may be considered mainstream, they all embrace the same overall belief system regarding evil. Though each expression of Buddhism interprets and practices particular aspects differently, a unified concept of evil emerges intact.

CHAPTER 7:

Identifying Key Components in the Systems of Evil

AFTER A CAREFUL ANALYSIS of the mainstream expressions of the world's major religions, all of these religions have either an explicit concept of evil or an implicit equivalent. The definitions of evil detailed in the preceding chapters have been arrived at through a variety of strategies: consideration of explicit philosophical and theological concepts, construction of concepts implied by antithesis and negation, reflection on the human experience of evil and suffering, or (most often) a combination of all of the aforementioned methods. Having concluded this portion of the study, the next step is to move toward identification of points for comparison and contrast.

In order to effectively analyze and identify the differences and similarities in religious thought regarding evil, one must thoroughly examine the key questions and core components of each system of thought. Examination of the religions in this study produced definitions of evil for each of these faiths. While there are major differences between these concepts of evil, there are similarities in terms of theme and the issues addressed by each belief system. Here they are phrased as questions that each system of evil answers for its adherents:

Is evil real or illusory?

What is the origin of evil?

Is there any human value from experiencing evil?

Can evil be conquered?

> If evil can be conquered, who is to do it?
>
> If evil can be conquered, how is it done?

While these questions are of universal concern in the religions under study, each religion gives drastically different answers—with one exception. Every religious system answers one question the same way: "Can evil be conquered?" This question has precisely the same answer in every belief system: "Yes." It is clearly a vital question that all religions attempt to answer for their respective adherents, and all of these religious systems teach that evil can indeed be conquered. Because of the agreement among religions on this question, it does not become a differentiating issue for analyzing and classifying religious systems of evil. Therefore, the question of whether or not evil can be conquered is not addressed with further analysis. Rather, the universal, affirmative answer to this question necessitates two deeper inquiries for the sake of understanding and classifying systems of evil with regard to the concept of conquering it: "*Who* defeats evil?" and "*How* is it defeated?"

In similar fashion, the two clarifying questions ("Who defeats evil?" and "How is it defeated?") are linked in their respective answers. "Who?" leads directly into "How?" One should not separate the questions and their answers. Therefore, this study combines the questions and answers under one heading in this section and in the subsequent system of classification (chapter 11: Conquering Evil).

As this book proceeds into this next phase, it will individually address every core question by analyzing each mainstream religion's concept of evil. This careful analysis of each system's answers will provide the detailed foundation that is necessary for developing a universal code of classification with regard to the concept of evil.

CHAPTER 8:

The Reality of Evil

The Reality of Evil in Judaism

JUDAIC SOURCES, THOUGH SOMETIMES reluctant to fully engage with the topic of theodicy, leave no room for disagreement as to whether or not evil is real or illusory. In Judaism, evil is undeniably real. For example, no mainstream sources deny that the Holocaust was real, and likewise these sources do not deny its deeply evil nature. Something that recent, impactful, and depraved stands out as a clear example of the reality of evil. The longtime suffering and persecution of Jews around the world, which took place throughout their entire history, lends further weight to this view.

Going beyond the recent widespread human experience of evil, Judaism acknowledges its reality in three ways. First, and of greatest importance, evil is real in actions that do not conform to the Torah's precepts (Cohen, 1995:96). Of secondary importance, the evil impulse is part of evil, which is something real as evidenced by God's creation of it and by its prevalence in human existence (Cohen, 1995:88; Heschel, 1976:365). Finally, and of least importance, evil is a reality as found in the spiritual forces of Satan and other evil spirits (Cohen, 1995:54-57, 260).

The Reality of Evil in Christianity

Christian thought seeks to avoid the dualistic tendencies, exemplified by the doctrines of the Jewish and Islamic impulses, by defining evil ontologically as a privation. God did not create the deficiency, absence, or corruption of God-ordained goodness, and therefore it may be tempting to label evil as something less than real in Christianity. Fernandes correctly identifies this as a core challenge for Christianity: how can evil be real, and how is it that something real does not come from God (2002a:123)? In addressing this concern, one should note that the essential nature of privation demonstrates that a privation does not originate with God. Privation is a lack or an absence, and God does not create privation; rather, the freedom God gave people creates the potential for privation (Geisler, 2002:46-47; Fernandes, 2000:14; Hines 2003:325). Evil is found when the *potential* for privation is *actualized* into an existential reality by human choice and behavior. While the actualization does not come from God, it is the actualization of a moral privation that makes evil a reality in human existence and experience. That God did not create actual evil (only the potential for privation) is not a concern, since privations are part of the reality of existence (Geisler, 2002:48; Boyd, 2003:63). Christian theology can point to its long, extensive collection of scriptures, theology, and practical attempts to diminish the impact of evil as evidence of evil's reality. It can also be argued that no one who experiences a privation would think that it is anything less than real. No mainstream Christian expression of theodicy denies the evil of the rape of a child, the ravages of an epidemic, or the horrible moral depravity of genocide. The individual who experiences blindness or deafness would not be tempted to consider those privations as anything other than very real and very impactful. For example, both the blind and the deaf sought Jesus' healing powers (Matthew 9:27-29; Mark 7:31-37). Spiritual forces could also cause suffering and evil that is very real.

Whether the evil is a metaphysical, moral, or physical privation, in both Christian theology and in the experiences of its adherents, evil is real. That God had no part in creating or actualizing evil in no way diminishes the reality of its existence or its impact on human experience.

The Reality of Evil in Islam

Islam takes the idea of evil in the lives of its adherents seriously. As detailed in chapter 4, evil is found in the spiritual influence of Iblis and the Jinn, in personal disbelief, in the choice of people to live imperfectly (even though perfection is fully within human reach), and in the suffering that results from failing to avoid evil urges. These things are all part of reality.

The intense call to social and governmental alignment with the divine revelation, as made clear and practical in the Sharia, is further evidence of the reality of evil in Islamic beliefs. One should note the number and strength of Quranic passages that offer individual solutions for evil, and one should also note the passages calling for governmental alignment with the divine will (Nasr, 2003:80, 110; Moaddel, 2002:379) as an aid against evil. The extensive regulations and pervasive guidance for overcoming evil implicitly demand its reality.

The Reality of Evil in Hinduism

Hinduism's answer as to whether or not evil is real or illusory requires careful analysis. Maya provides a key indicator of the correct way to approach this issue. The more-illusory-than-not nature of maya leads directly to (and plays a large role in) the concept of evil. It is undeniable that individuals struggle with both physical and mental roadblocks on their way to liberation. The evil things that hold back the self from knowing the Self include misperceptions, ignorance, pains caused to the non-actual self, and behaviors that reinforce the delusion of self.

All of these evil things point more to the illusory nature of evil than to the reality of evil.

Hinduism's lack of concern for the impact of one's activities provides another indicator of the correct answer to this question. Hinduism instructs an individual to be indifferent to results—success or failure, good or evil—and simply act without concern. This mandate goes so far as to teach that one is not to concern oneself with grief for death (Smith, H., 1991:31-32, 38-40; Fingarette, 1984:364; Shulman, 1979:668; Bhagavad Gita 2.6, 16, 19-21, 30, 50, 57, 3.18-19, 30, 4.14, 19-21, 5.10). By contrast, death is commonly thought of as an aspect of evil in theism. Hinduism labels the pain and suffering that result from one's actions (a classic way to define or judge evil) as unimportant, and this points to the human experience of evil as being illusory.

One finds another indicator regarding the reality of evil in Hinduism in the doctrine and origin of Buddhism. Buddhism sought to distinguish itself from Hinduism by acknowledging the reality of suffering (Gethin, 1998:59-60, 74; Das, 1998:199), as opposed to merely the illusion of suffering in Hinduism. This strongly indicates an illusory nature of suffering, which is a classic component of evil.

Nonetheless, as with many other aspects of the Hindu faith, the question of the reality of evil defies a strict either-or answer. While it may be tempting to label Hinduism as a system of pure illusion, this study accounts for the various aspects of evil, including human experience. Therefore, it is proper to consider the individual perception and experience of evil alongside the purely philosophical and theological. For example, if a Hindu caught in a house fire burns to death, it would be inappropriate to exclude that experience from consideration in this study. The self, though not the true Self, still perceives that it suffers grievously. It would be presumptuous to assume that a parent's grief suffered at the tragic death of a child is meaningless to a Hindu, even though the belief system claims the child's self did not truly matter as it was not the true Self. One might say that philosophically evil is illusory, but in the deluded experience of a human, suffering may feel very real and evil.

Evil, then, is not wholly illusory. It would be correct to say that it is more illusion than reality, perhaps far more so, but because of the experiences of the self, the answer must provide some acknowledgment of reality.

The Reality of Evil in Buddhism

Though it shares much with Hinduism, Buddhism offers a far easier answer to the question of the reality of evil. While the self is less-than-real in Buddhist thinking, it is not entirely nonexistent, and some limited value may be ascribed to the experiences of the self. The rejection of Hindu doctrines regarding indifference to outcomes and consequences allows the Buddhist to acknowledge the reality of an individual's suffering as well as the reality of its various sources (Goleman, 2003:79; Chen, 2001:26; Das, 1998:118-119; Gethin, 1998:78; Radhakrishnan & Moore, 1957:272). Even though there is no perpetual, intrinsic self in Buddhist thought, the individual's perception of a permanent self causes "dependent arising" (which is what leads to reincarnation), craving, and attachment. Furthermore, these things cause suffering for the causally connected, moment-to-moment aggregate that forms a person (Hershock, 2003:256; Scarborough, 2000:196-197; Keenan, 2002:142; Bond, 1980:240-241). While there is no perpetual self, the suffering of the impermanent self is viewed as real and worthy of concern. The breadth and depth of scripture, tradition, and literature allow one to see that while it may be difficult to comprehend the selfless self, Buddhism views evil, as defined by suffering and its cause, as real and pervasive in human experience.

CHAPTER 9:

The Origin of Evil

The Origin of Evil in Judaism

AS PART OF THE definition of evil in Judaism, the evil impulse poses a significant theological difficultly in Judaism with regard to the origin of evil (Satlow, 2003:216). The evil nature of the God-created evil impulse is not logically coherent when combined with the view that God remains good and separate from evil. To a large extent, the seeming contradiction of an all-good God creating the evil impulse appears to be handled by simply dismissing the problem and claiming that people cannot comprehend either evil or God's sovereign ways (and certainly not how the two interact with each other). Judaism does not offer an adequate solution for this dilemma, and Satlow acknowledges that the only possible way to resolve the issue is to say that the evil impulse really is not evil after all (2003:216), though this is logically contradictory and academically unsatisfactory.

One cannot escape the fact that Judaism clearly views God as the source of the impulses and spirits, both good and evil, even though He may be not the source of the correlative averot (Cohen, 1995:39, 88; Scherman & Zlotowitz, 1999:12, 15). The evil impulse, if unchecked (in expressing its purest form and unconditioned function), will lead to evil deeds. From the sources and analysis provided in chapter 2, it is clear that the evil impulse plays a significant role in the definition of evil in Judaism, and its source is God.

One should also take into account the human aspect of this topic. Human actions that do not conform to the Torah are evil and sinful (Cohen, 1995:96). Therefore, humans are a source of evil, even though God creates their evil impulse. In Judaic thought, human actions as a source of evil have greater weight than the evil impulse. When one allows the evil urge to actualize into action via one's failure to control it, he or she is fully condemned, even if it is expected. While God gives the evil urge to all people, Judaism teaches that people are able to please God with their actions and live righteously; therefore, the onus for individual acts of evil lies with the individuals.

With these things in mind, both God and humans are sources for things that are part of the broad definition of evil. Judaism gives responsibility for the source of evil to both God and humanity, but it is not an even split. When the various nuances are accounted for, the greater portion of the origin of evil lies with humanity.

The Origin of Evil in Christianity

Christianity also struggles with the problem of reconciling the seemingly contradictory doctrines of an all-powerful, all-loving God with the existence of evil in the world. Many struggle to understand how an omnipotent, omniscient God who works His divine will is not the source of the evils that plague His created world. Weatherhead made great progress in aiding Christian theology to confront evils in the form of trials, suffering, and sickness in conjunction with the will of God. He indicates that while God is indeed sovereign, He accomplishes His ultimate will *in spite of* the evils in the world; however, He is not the source of evil (1972:13-16). Suffering, then, is not part of the intentional will of God, but sometimes it is a part of what results from the circumstantial will of God working to accomplish His ultimate will. For example, God invited Hosea to a literal participation in a painful circumstance in order to enact a symbolic, prophetic analogy of Israel's unfaithfulness to God and bring corrective action and the potential for healing (Fiddes, 1993:175-176). In this example, Israel's unfaithfulness was the source of the painful circumstance, and the healing was God's will. In a New Testament example, Paul writes of his mysterious "thorn in the flesh" (2 Corinthians 12:7), but he refers to it as a circumstantial necessity to keep him humble, which implies an evil of pride sourced in his fallen nature, not in God (Russell, 1996:568; Ware, 2000:194-207).

The painful circumstances in life do not come from God. Rather, they result from original sin, which was a choice made in freedom by Adam (Schaeffer, 1968:81; Clendenin, 1988:326; Geisler, 2004:85-150). There was previously existing rebellion against God in the fall of Satan, but evil entered creation and brought the curse when Adam fell. At this point, sin corrupted human nature, and even creation suffers as a result. God is not responsible for evil in Christian thought. The fallen state of humanity and the world is the root of natural and physical evils, and the origin lies with humankind.

The Origin of Evil in Islam

Although Islam shares elements of the concept of evil with Judaism (such as the bad impulse), it finds a way to largely avoid the theological conundrum facing Judaic theology relating to God as a source of evil due to His creation of the impulse. Rather than ascribing metaphysical significance and theological importance to the impulse, Islam's evil impulse is of lesser importance when compared to Judaism. It is a mere mechanism that exposes the possibility of perfection—not a metaphysically significant force—and Islamic adherents are fully expected to overcome it and live perfectly (Ali, 1990:144). Because of Islam's evaluation of what actually constitutes an evil act (minor violations could circumstantially be viewed as eternally nonexistent), many theologically consistent Muslims may say that they have not really committed evil acts or truly succumbed to the bad impulse. Because of the unique way Islam approaches this topic, God's creation of the bad impulse has a minor role as a source of evil.

In Islamic thought, evil comes primarily, though not exclusively, from humans. The sin of disbelief is the origin of most of the evil in the world. The Quran re-enables forgetful humanity to avoid evil, so the primary source of evil is in human actions that ignore the enabling revelation. The exception to this is the experiential aspect of trials and suffering sent by God to test people and lead them toward perfection (Watt, 1979:18-19; Farah, 2003:123; Ali 1990:144, 253-254).

The Origin of Evil in Hinduism

When determining the source of evil in Hinduism, one faces challenges that are very similar to those faced when attempting to define the level of reality in the Hindu concept of evil. If all is Brahman, and if evil is real, then one might naturally assume that evil would originate from the Brahman. However, earlier portions of this study have already established that evil is more illusion than it is real, and therefore the question moves toward identifying the source of the illusion of evil and of the human experiences resulting from the delusory existence of self. From the perspective of evil as delusion, misperception, and undesirable actions that do not comply with dharma, one finds its source in each individual self but not the ultimate, unified Self. The delusion, misguided actions, and incorrect thoughts come from humanity's lack of perceiving the true, Brahmanic nature of existence (Gita 2.62-65). Therefore, because humans incorrectly perceive true existence, it would be easy to conclude that the origin of Hindu evil comes strictly from humans. This is further supported by the various scriptures indicating that the realization of truth leads to freedom from sorrow and liberation (Kena Upanishad IV:9; Mundaka Upanishad III:2-3).

However, the Hindu concept of maya complicates this conclusion. Maya is a significant contributor to the discussion of the origin of evil since it is the material veil of non-reality that keeps people in their delusion and hinders them from truth and enlightenment (Moran, 2001:37; Michaels, 2004:263), which would relieve evil and suffering of the perceived self. As maya emanates from the God-Brahman, one may point to the Divine as being the source of evil in Hinduism. Going further, the significance of the role of maya is such that if there were no maya, humans would not struggle with delusion of self and individuality, and they would instead proceed straight to enlightenment and freedom from the Hindu equivalent of evil. Instead, people must work to destroy the illusion of maya and seek perfection that is free from its influence (Morgan, 2001:37, 53).

Once more with Hinduism, a clearly delineated answer does not present itself in the form of an easy absolute. If one takes into account all the perspectives of this study, both the humans and the Divine share responsibility for the source of evil (which is really the source of delusion). However, when one considers the overall significance of maya and its impact on this topic, one should give greater weight to the Divine and the role of maya in deluding humanity, and a lesser portion of responsibility for the origin of evil lies with the misguided selves of humanity.

The Origin of Evil in Buddhism

In mainstream Buddhist doctrine, evil has a specific, defined source. Understanding the origin of evil is a vital part of Buddhist practice, and it is key for dealing with the problem on an individual level. Therefore, the topic of identifying and understanding the source of evil is a common topic in Buddhist literature (Das, 1998; Gethin, 1998; Goleman, 2003).

The portion of Buddhist scriptures called the *Majjhima-nikaya* introduces the origin of evil: "And what is the origin of suffering? It is craving, which brings renewal of being, is accompanied by delight and lust, and delights in this and that; that is, craving for sensual pleasures, craving for being, and craving for non-being. This is called the origin of suffering" (MN 9 v. 16).

Going further than just stating that craving is the source of evil, the concept of the "Three Poisons" explains Buddhist thought on how evil arises. Also known as negative or destructive emotions, these poisons are the three categories of negative thought that perpetuate an individual's delusion and cause suffering. The word poison accurately implies the seriousness of the issue: a constant, insidious, destructive process that Buddhism claims afflicts all people (Keenan, 2002:142; Wayman, 1957:107-109; Das, 1998:58). Ignorance, attachment, and aversions are the poisons that also function as sources of evil.

The first poison is *ignorance of the truth*. If one does not truly exist as a permanent, perpetual self, then the delusion of existence sustained by ignorance can only lead to increasing trouble and pain. The changing nature of existence is something people are unaware of, and they base their lives on a view that embraces the permanence of selfhood. Since the view of permanence is flawed, and since people rely upon it, it follows naturally that undesirable things are the result of this mismatch between perception and reality. This is heavily dependent on the interaction between human life and dukkha (Fonner, 1993:5; Smart, 1984:371-372; Gethin, 1998:61; Das, 1998:77, 329; Ryan, 2003:144).

The second poison is *attachment*. It is born out of the previous poison of ignorance, and as such, it builds upon the delusion of selfhood. When acting in ignorance, an individual craves things for his or her self, and then he or she forms attachments to those things. These cravings and attachments serve only to perpetuate the delusion as well as to make an individual more vulnerable to suffering when change takes place. Change is unpleasant, or worse, it is devastating.

Even once a person has become accustomed to a new circumstance that has resulted from change, things will change again, and the individual will experience pain again. In the end, the individual develops *aversions* (the third poison) to things, people, objects, mind-sets, or circumstances that he or she perceives to precipitate pain or change (Burton, 2002:326; Keenan, 2002:142; Hershock, 2003:256; Scarborough, 2000:196-197).

These aversions are the negative or destructive emotions that develop as a direct result of the pain and suffering that one has experienced. They are an inevitable result of previously developed cravings and attachments. They induce more suffering and are significant roadblocks to achieving enlightenment. Because of the finite, transitory, changing nature of the world, people end up not experiencing the things they desire, and they develop aversions to those things perceived to be the cause of their lack (Gethin, 1998:70; Das, 1998:82-83; Goleman, 2003:79). Because of their aversions, negative or destructive emotions develop. Building upon ignorance and attachment, experiences of change or lack cause people to hurt, and then emotions such as hate, anger, and disappointment emerge in an individual (Das, 1998:60).

By analyzing Buddhist writings, one can see that suffering comes from human craving, and the craving comes from ignorance. Both attachments and aversions strengthen it. It perpetuates beyond death through reincarnation, which itself results from a person's delusory conditioned existence and the craving to satisfy the delusory desires that are not compatible with the true nature of existence (Hershock, 2003:256; Scarborough, 2000:196-197). It is important to note that there is no original sin in Buddhist doctrine as the concept of a Buddha-nature and core emptiness precludes assigning such a judgment. One can logically discern this from the common Buddhist view that the nature of the absolute reality itself transcends these concepts (Buri & Oliver, 1992:98; Buddhadasa, 1989:234).

With the preceding views taken into account, one can now discern the source of evil. As Buddhism is non-theistic, and as the source of evil is in human views and behaviors, it should be clear that evil's origin comes from human craving, ignorance, attachment, and aversions. Humanity is the source of its own evils.

CHAPTER 10:

Value in the Human Experience of Evil

Judaism's Assessment of Value in the Human Experience of Evil

IN JUDAIC THOUGHT REGARDING the origin of evil, it is God who created the evil impulse (Cohen, 1995:88). This impulse is necessary for humanity's survival, so the easy approach would be to claim that there is great value in the human experience of evil (Ariel, 1995:86-87). However, this would be simplistic and incorrect, and avoiding this potential error requires careful focus. The real query at the heart of this issue is not whether there is value in evil or its source; rather, it is a question of whether or not there is value in the *human experience* of evil. This is by nature an experiential topic. When one suffers, particularly if that suffering is undeserved, it is a common response to ask not only why one suffers, but also if there is any value in the suffering. This natural human tendency looks for hope and optimism in circumstances that might otherwise lead one to hopelessness.

Evil is experienced when a person suffers consequences of an averah that he or she has committed (Cohen, 1005:111, 116) or that societal behavior has caused (Cohen, 1995:44-45, 216). Alternatively, suffering may be due to some natural or physical evil that does not appear to be the direct result of a personal averah, such as the death of Job's family and servants from a Sabean attack, from three Chaldean raiding parties, by fire from the sky, and by a mighty wind (Job 1:13-20). Another example of this is the experience of the Jews in the Nazi concentration camps. Some could attempt to claim that persecutions such as these serve to enhance character and to develop positive attributes. However, the torture, starvation, and attempted mass extermination of an entire race served no good purpose either directly or indirectly, determinatively or non-determinatively. In his consideration of evil, which the Holocaust largely influenced, Fackenheim leaves no room to question the worthlessness of such an experience: "It did not enhance the humanity of its inhabitants. On the contrary, it was single-mindedly geared to the destruction of the humanity (as well as the lives) of the victims" (1985:514). In Judaism, while there is value in resisting evil, there is nothing for an individual to gain from the experience of the extreme forms of evil such as the Holocaust.

There are some other common views of the experience of suffering in Judaic thought. In one scenario, limited forms of suffering are God's corrective action toward a wayward individual and may cause that individual to turn to the Torah (Cohen, 1995:118-119). However, it has little pure value on its own, other than indicating that one may be an object of His grace since the righteous often suffer in this world (Carmy, 1999:12; Cohen, 1995:111; Ariel, 1995:102). Otherwise, there is no human value in the experience. Another common theme is that suffering may be indicative of one's spiritual state (such as righteous or unrighteous). The righteous suffer because they have embraced a righteous lifestyle, which is intrinsically difficult, and perhaps suffering is naturally a part of existing under God's plan and in His grace (Lichtenstein, 1999:45). Regardless of the different views, in the Judaic mind, suffering as indicative of a state of righteousness is of little value. The most that one may gain is that the suffering may confirm to one that he or she is already righteous; it does not increase one's righteousness. The value is not in the experience of suffering itself.

When one focuses on the human experience of suffering, there may be some potentially positive value in terms of drawing one closer to God (Cohen, 1995:118-119) or in developing positive attributes, though it is not a point of emphasis and should not be overvalued. Suffering can also produce the potential for good things, such as earning merit through resistance to evil as evil is something God expects humankind to resist (Steinberg, 1975:57; Cohen, 1995:96). However, in an experiential context, value is ascribed to actuality and not potentiality. Hence, far greater value would be associated with the *resistance* to evil than to the human *experience* of evil. In the final analysis, much of the human experience of suffering is ultimately meaningless in and of itself.

Christianity's Assessment of Value in the Human Experience of Evil

Evil, suffering, and trials are not part of God's intentional will in mainstream, Christian theodicy. The paradox is that some suffering can be considered good based on the context surrounding it. Some suffering also results from positively addressing or correcting a previously unhealthy or corrupt spiritual state. Lewis describes how God allows pain and suffering in order to bring spiritual healing (2001:43). Others point out that suffering is the personal, experiential knowledge of sin, and as such, it can help an individual seek God by increasing personal humility and decreasing one's focus on oneself (Bonhoeffer, 1997:135; Kronke, 2004:22, 27). This is similar to the example of someone who has cancer. Painful suffering may result from surgical procedures, radiation, and chemotherapy; however, these treatments are good things that not only improve the person's overall health, they help the person to continue living. These particular human experiences of suffering both are good and lead to goodness; therefore, in this context, and to the extent that they produce good, there is some value that one can gain from suffering.

In addition, people can only develop certain moral attributes by experiencing difficult circumstances. Patience requires long-suffering and trials, and one can claim that the formulation of attributes such as patience makes the world a morally superior place. This reinforces the Christianity theology in which God promises the believer He will bring something good out of the experience of evil circumstances and suffering (Romans 8:28; Fiddes, 1993:186; Geisler, 2002:58, 347; Ware, 2000:192-193; Henry, 1999:304). This indicates neither the intentional will of God in creating the suffering nor a change in the basic nature of evil. Rather, it teaches that a truly sovereign, loving, and omniscient God will exercise His divine omnipotence to bring something positive out of the human experience of evil. This does not redeem the situation or the cause, but it does promise the believer that God will always cause some value to arise from his or her personal experience of evil circumstances.

Islam's Assessment of Value in the Human Experience of Evil

Islam offers two answers to the question of whether or not there is value in the human experience of evil. First, the human choice to ignore the divine revelation and engage in acts of evil produces no significant value, and there is no significant value in the resultant suffering. This view is consistent with the expectation that all people can live perfectly (Sharif, 1959:42; Ali, 1990:175, 181, 193). However, this is specific to the evil resulting from free-will choices of humanity.

Alternatively, Islam acknowledges the experience of evil in the form of suffering and trials that come from God. In this view, the experience of evil is something that moves people toward perfection, and it is part of the divine plan to develop strong, desirable attributes. In fact, some teach that the greatest and holiest people experience the greatest suffering (Watt, 1070:18-19; Farah, 2003:123; Ali, 1990:144, 253-254). However, it is difficult to call the trials that specifically come from God truly evil when they lead an individual toward perfection.

Therefore, one may not offer a simple yes or no answer as to whether or not there is value in the human experience of evil according to the Islamic view. The proper answer is to claim that there can be value in the human experience of evil, but both the basic value and the magnitude of any potential value is subject to the circumstances, and any value one can gain is limited.

Hinduism's Assessment of Value in the Human Experience of Evil

In investigating this topic, it may be tempting to look at the role of karma in the human experience of supposed evils. The popular argument in this line of thought says that the human experience of various evils is of great value as these experiences serve to expiate bad karma, which in turns elevates one closer to unity with the Brahman. However, Hindu sources (cited in Chapter 5) clearly reveal that these karmically induced circumstances and experiences are part of what is evil; therefore, one cannot base an argument for human value in the experience of evil on karma. In avoiding this popular pitfall, one must carefully look to the human experience of illusion, misperception, and misguided actions that reinforce duality and self at the expense of unity and Self. Therefore, one must ask what value there is in the human experience of delusion. There are two points to make with this approach.

First, the delusory nature of both existence and perception renders the ascription of value to any perceived experience (including experiences of evil and suffering) intrinsically flawed. Any human action, which has its impetus in preceding human perception, as well as one's perception of the action are flawed. Therefore, it is difficult to judge the accuracy of ascribed value in this scenario. Any value judgment is at risk of being intrinsically delusory.

Second, any value ascribed to a delusory experience or perception serves to reinforce the delusion and reinforces the evil itself. This serves no greater purpose and offers no benefit. If the self perceives that it is suffering from physical pain, then that experience reinforces self at the expense of Self as the self seeks to separate itself from the perceived cause of the pain. The perpetuation of the belief in and emphasis on self as opposed to Self is a downward spiral and offers no true value in the Hindu system. Therefore, there is no value for the Hindu adherent in the human experience of evil.

Buddhism's Assessment of Value in the Human Experience of Evil

Suffering is undesirable in Buddhism, and Buddhism seeks to eliminate it (Gethin, 1998:59; Das, 1998:199). One of the largest problems for an adherent is the multitude of things that reinforce attachment, aversion, ignorance, and craving (Gethin, 1998:71, 74; Das, 1998:58-60). The experience of suffering does not lead one toward enlightenment; instead, it will often strengthen that which ought to be diminished, and this is the third poison of aversion (Das, 1998:60). As with Hinduism, the experience of suffering is more likely to worsen things than to make them better as it reinforces the sense of a perpetual self. However, there is the possibility that extreme attachment and aversion will cause some individuals to recoil from the misperception of a perpetual self and pursue a more acceptable middle ground, so the possibility, though not the likelihood, for some very small value does exist. Nevertheless, the overall assessment of value in the human experience of evil falls well on the side of not providing value.

CHAPTER 11:

Conquering Evil

THE FINAL QUESTION IN this chapter requires a more detailed analysis than the preceding questions. First, the basic question of whether or not evil can be conquered is affirmative in all religions, which necessitates that two subsequent differentiating questions be dealt with in this section: Who conquers evil and how is evil conquered? This section covers both of these questions. Second, these questions delve deeply into each religion's respective doctrines of evil, redemption, soteriology, eschatology, and other germane areas, and proper analysis and exposition necessitates a deeper review that covers a broad spectrum of theological topics within each religion. There may be no more central issue to religion than dealing with overcoming evil, injustice, and suffering (Yinger, 1977:72).

Judaism's Approach to Conquering Evil

Judaism claims that it is the duty of each individual to conquer evil in his or her life, and it is within each individual's ability to do so, aided by the Torah and by performing *mitvot* (singular: mitzvah; Heschel, 1976:375-377; Ariel, 1995:88; Cohen, 1995:91-92). God considers people worthy of His redemptive acts only if they conquer the evil impulse and follow His will as revealed in the Torah (Heschel, 1976:348, 379-380; Ariel, 1995:159). When an individual conquers the evil impulse, evil actions will not occur. Likewise, the experiential consequences of averot will not materialize if no evil act occurs in the first place. Humankind can also resist Satan and evil spirits aided by the Torah (Cohen, 1995:58). After reviewing these initial basic doctrines of Judaism, it appears that if evil is to be conquered, humanity will have to accomplish it.

The Torah is the key to humanity's ability to conquer evil. Regardless of whether one makes use of traditional or modern views, there is a consistent, overall, mainstream view of the Torah as summarized in four points. First, the Torah is widely regarded as pre-existing creation, and it is perfect in its original, divine form, even though humans may not always interpret it correctly (Cohen 1995:104, 131-133, 347; Heschel, 1976:244). Second, any subsequent claim of authoritative interpretation or inspiration must be consistent with the original, divine revelation given to Moses. Subsequent interpretation cannot introduce clear contradictions (Dozeman, 2000:29-30; Levenson, 2000-2001:40-41; Spero, 1986: 79-90). Third, the subsequent Talmudic interpretations of the Torah have a special role as they have provided unity and cohesiveness for the divergent aspects of Judaism during the past two thousand years, and they often serve as a framework for future interpretations of the Torah (Wald & Martinez, 2001:380; Schiffman, 2000:156-157). Fourth, all forms of mainstream Judaism recognize (in some form) that the 613 precepts consisting of 365 prohibitions and 248 commandments reveal God's guidelines for human well-being.

The Torah is the revelation of God's way for humans to live. Deliberate internalization and careful study of the Torah helps control, channel, and cure the evil impulse, and it helps gradually create personal improvement and good actions in one's life (Satlow, 2003:110;

Ben-Menahem, 2002:22-23; Ariel, 1995:86; Cohen, 1995:91-93). For example, one thirteenth-century prayer petitions God to enlighten the way of obedience, to make the Torah increase in importance for one's children, and to increase the number of good deeds performed (Langermann, 2001:134). This serves as another indicator of the role of the Torah in conquering evil.

Jewish analysis of the Book of Job emphasizes the struggle to resist evil impulses and circumstances of suffering while maintaining integrity. In this story, the suffering is the catalyst by which Job is able to perform good deeds and make declarations of faith. Job's suffering is not something that demands a justification of God (Steinmann, 1996:89-91; Fleming, 1994:481). Evil is to be conquered by humanity, and no explanation beyond that is necessary. When considering evil and suffering, the Halakhic approach moves the emphasis from philosophy and toward individual responsibility as well as practical, human responses to evil. It is unnecessary to inquire as to the cause of evil, but empathetic, action-oriented living toward others who suffer and experience evil is part of the solution (Sokol, 1999:311-323). This emphasis on practical, human action is entirely consistent with the conclusion that Judaism teaches that human deeds in conformity with the Torah are the key ingredient in conquering evil in one's life.

The mental internalization of the Torah goes together with two other important parts of an individual's ability to counter evil: right intention and proper contrition. One must not only follow the Torah with his or her deeds, but one's intentions in performing deeds must come from a relatively pure desire to follow God's guidance for the sake of what is right or even to repay God for His greatness (Ehrlich, 2003:38; Stadler, 2002:466; Heschel, 1976:306-307, 387, 403-404). An individual can have an overall right intention and a love of the Torah even though a particular averah may manifest itself in an apparent contradiction. Perfection, while the goal, is not required; however, contrition for failure is vital. One will have both right intention and proper contrition if the Torah holds a central place in the heart (Brener, 2004:219; Heschel, 1976:402-403).

One should note that right intention only has value to the extent that one's actions properly actualize it. There is some acknowledgment in Judaism that human efforts may fail to conquer evil no matter how good the intentions behind the efforts. The imperfection of the human mind and the lack of human foreknowledge both contribute to this idea. People's plans may not be the same as God's plan for them in resisting evil, as was evidenced by several stories in scripture (Murphy, 1986:5-14). Examples found outside of scripture also demonstrate this. The two examples of Rudolph Kastner and the Union Générale des Israélites de France both illustrate that poor outcomes may nullify good intentions. Kastner's intention to aid fellow Jews against the Nazis failed miserably. He was charged with evil action and self-serving favoritism, he was compared to Faust, and one judge even labelled him as a Trojan horse (Bilsky, 2004:117-160). Eventually one of the Holocaust survivors assassinated Kastner. In a different example, some residents of France wanted to aid the Jews suffering under the German occupation, and so they formed the Union Générale des Israélites de France. However, the organization was subverted and ended up becoming a tool of the Nazis by which they advanced their persecution of the Jews. In the end, the council appears to have made the evil acts of the Nazis easier to accomplish, which was the opposite of the council's good intention (Marrus, 1987:317-318). In these two examples, evil triumphed, and despite people's good intentions and careful plans, no one earned merit for these well-intended, but ultimately disastrous, deeds.

When good intentions result in good outcomes, people earn merit toward redemption. Earning merit is important since this is what makes one worthy of redemption. Some teachings indicate that performing a good deed that one is commanded to perform is of greater value than performing a deed that is one is not explicitly commanded to perform (Benatar, 2002:6-8). This view further increases the importance of the Torah and its 613 precepts. Going further, the Hiddur Mitzvah demonstrates the importance of works in earning merit. Its principle is that if one truly loves the Torah, then one can earn extra merit by exceeding the basic, minimum requirements of the precept, and it can be as simple as bringing food to the grieving bereaved on one's most beautiful and extravagant dishes. However, in order to limit poor judgment and harmful excess, the rabbis determined that the extra merit earned could only extend one-third beyond the original value (Brener, 2004:243; Katz, 1995:128; Greene, 1992:36; Cohen, 1995:150-151).

While the Torah guides the individual and his or her deeds for the defeat of personal evil, God will defeat some evils Himself in an eschatological solution. This is Judaism's final solution to the problem of evil: God conquers the evil that humans could not. This includes the elimination of metaphysical evils such as Satan and evil spirits. While God expects humans to successfully resist those evils (and merit God's favor by doing so), individuals cannot ultimately conquer (eliminate) these final evils, and they serve no purpose other than to destroy humanity (Steinberg, 1975:57; Fackenheim, 1985:514, 1982:113-130).

The Messiah plays a large role in the eschatological views of Judaism. In traditional expressions, while individuals are directly responsible for dealing with personal evil, the arrival of the Messiah heralds God's eschatological triumph over evil as the Messiah redeems the world by eliminating the evils that humans could not conquer. A time of complete peace, joy, and love follows. He will rebuild what was ruined, bring all of nature into harmony, and death will be vanquished (Cohen, 1995:352-353; Steinberg, 1975:168; Heschel, 1976:379).

The world to come is the place of the human afterlife. Once the righteous have entered the world to come, the physical activities that were previously a part of human existence are no longer necessary; therefore, humanity no longer requires the evil impulse to provide the energy to do those things. Therefore, God fully purges the evil impulse and the evil spirits, and they will plague people no more (Cohen, 1995:92; Heschel, 1976:379). Thus, the elimination of the impulse conquers this portion of evil.

When analyzing who is responsible for conquering evil, one must remember that the righteous *earn* their way into the world to come by their actions. God performs the elimination of the evil impulse, but because God does not remove the impulse until after people have earned their entrance to the world to come, the greater soteriological responsibility for conquering evil lies with humans. After all, redemption is a result of humankind having made itself and the world worthy of redemption (Heschel, 1976:348, 379-380; Ariel, 1995:92, 159).

The emphasis on human responsibility only grows when one considers modern forms of Judaism. The eschatological views of the Messiah and the world to come are considered literal by traditionalists, but many of those who embrace modern expressions of Judaism view these eschatological items as symbolic for human growth and achievement (Steinberg, 1975:170). There may be no literal Messiah, and there may be no world to come; rather, humanity is its own Messiah as it delivers itself and in doing so creates a better, righteous world.

Regardless of which perspective one embraces, the role of God in defeating evil is a smaller role than that of humanity. While He does play a limited role, the greater portion of responsibility lies with humanity. Therefore, it is appropriate to claim that the majority of responsibility for the defeat of evil lies with humanity, and they accomplish the defeat of evil by actualizing the commands of the Torah into action in their everyday lives.

Christianity's Approach to Conquering Evil

A core doctrine of Christianity is the utter inability of humanity to conquer evil. Human nature is corrupt, and people are unable to avoid sin and evil. Creation itself also suffers from evil and corruption, and that lies outside the ability of humans to correct. Many passages in the Bible instruct people to do things that appear related to deed-based conquering of evil and suffering, such as the command to take care of widows and orphans (James 1:17) and the powerful humility of the beatitudes (Matthew 5:1-16). However, at the most these are instructions for the faithful to engage with people and show them sacrificial compassion that points to the goodness of God. They are not indicators that human efforts will conquer evil.

Christian theology offers the world a new approach to theodicy by virtue of its doctrine of the Incarnation. Jesus, the second person of the Trinity, is God incarnate, and He is fully human and fully God. As God incarnate, Jesus gives Christian theology the unique opportunity to see God's will toward evil and human suffering firsthand. Jesus reveals God's tenderness and compassion for suffering people not only by preaching for the sake of the salvation of people's souls, but also by the physical healing of those who are sick and suffering (John 4:43-54; Matthew 4:32-25, 8:1-4, 14-17; Mark, 1:29-34, 40-45; Luke 4:38-41, 5:12-16). He was not concerned merely with eternal salvation; His actions as God incarnate demonstrated that He was anything but detached and indifferent to the human experience of evil (Boyd, 2003:14-15). Also, Christ's compassionate involvement with and healing of those who suffer is an expression of God's will (healing, compassion, love) as opposed to the false view that His direct, intentional will is that people be sick and suffer for some mysterious purpose that is only known to God (Boyd, 2003:51). The Christian view, as supported by the earthly actions of God incarnate, proclaims that He wants to heal and to restore. God is not a passive observer. He remains deeply committed to and involved with

His creation, and He will use evil and suffering for the good of believers (Wright, 2006:40; Pinnock, 1994:101-102; Birch, 2003:145-150; Phillips, 1991:111; Henry, 1999:303). In this regard, evil, as the human experience of suffering, is something God allows but is able to conquer.

Another unique aspect to Christian theodicy is the claim that evil has actually been defeated in an objective, historical event, but that the full implementation and practical realization of the victory will not arrive until the final judgment. This starts with Christ's sacrifice and resurrection. God is not the source of evil, but He took the responsibility for its defeat squarely upon His shoulders when Jesus died on the cross. This accomplished God's ultimate will, and it showed just how deeply involved He is. It is also the Christian's guarantee of the defeat of evil (Weatherhead, 1972:15; Rice, 1994:44-46; Henry, 1999:304; Flora, 1992:15; Clendenin, 1988:325-326). Some theologians offer up this unique solution to evil as superior evidence that evil has already been defeated. The doctrine of a God who shares in human suffering satisfies the question of the justice of God. Christ's sacrifice on the cross (along with His subsequent resurrection) was an evil-conquering event that took place in historical time, something that is unique among the world's religions. As such, this historical act of God is the only reliable guarantee and reason for humans to hope that life will someday be completely free from evil (Surin, 1983:246-247; Fernandes, 2000:12-14).

One can find the culmination of Christianity's defeat of evil in its eschatology. As with some other faiths, Christian theology looks toward a final judgment and the heavenly afterlife that follows it. While Christianity teaches that Christ's sacrifice and resurrection won the victory over evil, God accomplishes the full implementation of that victory in His perfect (future) timing. When this point in time is reached and God's plan is revealed in its fullness, the justice of God will be clear, even to those who are condemned, and the faithful will inhabit the freshly revealed new heaven and earth (Revelation 21:1). In this final, full implementation of victory, nothing corrupt, sinful, or evil will remain, and the creation itself, which suffered so brutally because of the Fall, will be renewed and perfected. God forever eliminates Satan and evil from the lives of believing humanity. God casts Satan and the spirits into the Lake of Fire for eternity. Unbelievers also experience the just wrath of God and His punishment against sin in hell (Grudem, 1994:1146-1147, 1163; Erickson, 1998:1236; Althaus, 1966:418-421; Wright, 2006:165). While many theologians focus on the Christological component of God's conquering of evil, Osborne emphasizes the eschatological solution as an appropriate and necessary part (1993:64-65). The details of Christian eschatology continue to reinforce the Christian idea that humanity cannot conquer evil—God must conquer it.

Islam's Approach to Conquering Evil

Human perfection is expected and demanded in Islam. Therefore, whether at the personal or societal level, the responsibility for overcoming evil lies mainly with humanity. Human and societal conformity to the will of God as expressed through the Quran and the Sharia achieve this. As evil generally has its genesis in one's own actions, which need not even lead to evil in the first place, the duties of the Muslim lead away from evil and toward perfection. The perfect, divine revelation of the Quran enables humankind to overcome forgetfulness, disbelief, and imperfection. Furthermore, a choice to believe and act in accordance with God's decrees results in a divinely reinforced cycle that will make it increasingly easier to overcome evil (the reverse is also true). The five pillars, prayer, and the purity of one's faith are a few examples of behaviors that lead away from evil and aids one in overcoming the bad impulse (Nasr 2002:132; Ali, 1990:263-267; Farah, 2003:134-135; Juynboll 2001:331). The Sharia plays a critical role as well since it presents Muslim law and proper behavior not only for the individual, but also for society as a whole. Conformity to God's revealed will in human action is how evil is defeated (or perhaps more properly, avoided).

The Islamic devotee who attempts to overcome evil will embrace the five pillars of the Islamic faith, and these pillars consist of belief in the one, true God (though it is a belief made manifest by action via public declaration) and four actions. These actions are: daily prayers, tithe, fasting, and the famous pilgrimage that all believers are to make at least once during their lifetime (Moosa, 2000:192; Janin & Kahlmeyer, 2007:15). The purity of an individual's faith, as exemplified by the pillars, will aid one in refraining from the temptation of sin (Juynboll, 2001:331). Disciplined, sincere following of the five pillars will aid one in achieving perfection and conquering personal evil. However, the concepts of perfection, sin, and evil are influenced by Islam's unique approach (limited mutability) to these topics, and as a result, perfection does not carry the same exacting connotation that is seen in other theistic faiths.

The Quran is the primary guide for Muslim activities in response to the potential and actuality of evil in the world. However, as Islam encourages analysis and discourse in determining right living, the *Sunnah* and the *Hadith* play major roles in discovering practical, experiential ways to combat evil. The Sunnah is the sayings of the Prophet, and the Hadith is the recorded doings of the Prophet. People often refer to them collectively as one or the other. Regardless of title, it is second only to the Quran as an authoritative guide on Islamic life, which includes laws and government (Ali, 1990:44; Nasr, 2003:99; Farah, 2003:36; Mumisa, 2002:55-57; Janin & Kahlmeyer, 2007:19). The Sharia emerges from this great tradition, and it is the Islamic interpretation of God's will made explicit in the form of Islamic law. It describes the way to good living, proper values, right spirituality, and the rights and obligations of a proper, Islamic society (Mohammad, 1985:384; Moosa, 2000-2001:193; Janin & Kahlmeyer, 2007:1, Gordon, 2003:110-111). In practice, much of

Islam is based on this divinely revealed law, and in it there is almost no separation between religious and secular domains as its goal is to conform society to match the will of God in doing good and overcoming evil (Chipman, 2001:6; Nasr, 2003:80, 110; Nasr, 2002:117-119).

The Sharia has a determined hierarchy of authority that all Sunni Muslims follow (Shi'ites have a slightly different hierarchy for divine law, but it is similar). In descending order, the hierarchy is as follows: The Quran, the Sunnah (referring collectively to the Sunnah and the Hadith), *qiyas* (human reason, logic, and analysis), and *ijma*, which is the general consensus of the Islamic society (Metzger, 1994-1995:697-714; Mumisa, 2002:15; Mohammad, 1985:384). If it is followed perfectly, the Sharia will lead the individual to heaven in addition to having a transformative effect on the society in which one lives (Janin & Kahlmeyer, 2007:1; Nasr, 2002:119-120). The people of the world do good and conquer (avoid) evil if they follow and fully implement the Sharia. The politicization of Islam is the *praxis* of Islamic theology. Islam teaches that humankind is forgetful, not sinful (Nasr, 2003:65; Smith H., 1989:239). God's revelation remedies that forgetfulness, and this enables humankind to live and work toward perfection. One must completely surrender to the divine will, and as the divine will combines spiritual and natural law in God's decree for the world, the good works of people must extend to encompass society and government with no separation between divine and secular law (Nasr, 2003:110; Moosa, 2000-2001:187; Moaddel, 2002:379; Houben, 2003:149). Thus, human efforts in these collective forms are also part of the solution to evil.

Islam makes it clear that humanity must conquer evil. Adherence to the Quran and studying the Sunnah and the Hadith enable individuals to conquer evil. Society and government must also work to conquer evil, and the Sharia provides the practical guidelines for conforming society to the will of God (Nasr, 2003:80). However, the end of evil in the form of trials and suffering inflicted upon people for their own benefit comes in an eschatological solution (as there is no longer any need for those trials in eternity). To this extent, some small portion of the responsibility for defeating evil lies with God as He stops sending these trials. Nevertheless, the vast majority of responsibility lies with humanity and in how well people implement Islamic beliefs and laws in their personal lives as well as in society.

Hinduism's Approach to Conquering Evil

Hinduism offers a clearly delineated approach to conquering evil. The individual self must engage in the pursuit of enlightenment through the four *yogas* (see below). *Moksha*, the Hindu victory over evil (when the delusion of self is conquered and the unitive state is gained), is the end result of individual, human efforts spent pursuing the yogas in an attempt to diminish an individual's sense of self and increase intuitive realization of Self (Narayanan, 2003:139; Renard, 2002:257; Michaels, 2004:19; Morgan, 2001:18). While the law of karma is part of the ultimate reality of the Brahman, the responsibility to conquer the illusory nature of self lies with each adherent. Therefore, each individual is responsible for conquering his or her own evil—karma and the Brahman will not conquer evil for the Hindu. The individual's defeat of evil will make use of at least one of the four yogas: *Raja Yoga* (the path of mental and physical discipline), *Karma Yoga* (the path of action and deeds), *Jnana Yoga* (the path of knowledge), and *Bhakti Yoga* (the path of individual devotion). Only through an individual's careful, directed discipline will evil be defeated. Since the paths are not exclusive, a Hindu may take advantage of several, although most adherents focus their energies on a single path. A superficial survey of the paths may appear to indicate a severe disparity in underlying philosophy and approach; however, the end goal is the same (moksha, unitive state) regardless of the path chosen. An individual accomplishes this goal by practices aimed at decreasing the sense of the individual self and increasing the intuitive realization of the unitive Self-Atman-Brahman (Narayanan, 2003:139; Renard, 2002:257; Michaels, 2004:19; Morgan, 2001:18; Smith, H., 1991:26-29, 50). When one thinks of Hinduism, one may think of the ascetic hermit, the person trying to balance deeds and karma, the disciplined, meditating yogi, or the individual who is fervently devoted to an individual manifestation of one of the gods. All of these paths, properly understood, de-emphasize self by leading the devoted adherent to Atman-Brahman and the unitive state, thus; a personal conquering of evil.

Of all these paths, perhaps the most well-known is the path of individual devotion (Bhakti Yoga). This path teaches that since all gods are manifestations of the singular ultimate reality, any sincere devotion to any specific god is devotion to the singular God-Brahman (Miller, 2001:35; Morgan, 2001:71; Smith, H., 1991:34-36; Narayanan, 2003:140, 145; Renard, 2002:262). Sincere devotion is the key. As an example of sincere devotion along this line of thought, during a Vedic soma sacrifice that took place in London in 1996, the *soma* (a ritual drink) was spontaneously worshipped by priests and lay people (Smith, F., 2000:256-257). In this instance, the worshippers expressed the unity of all things with the Brahman through their genuine, heartfelt worship of a bottle of liquid. Thus, the worship of a somatic representation of Vishnu is direct worship of Vishnu (Sheth, 2002:110). The worshippers in London viewed the object as a single entity, "Vishnu-Brahman-soma." Even though different devotees worship different deities, the ultimate goal of devotion remains the unitive state (Morgan, 2001:71; Smith, H., 1991:26, 62). This is a truth that is easily lost, and complete devotion—which is *self*less—leads to liberation and unity (Nath, 2001:42; Narayanan, 2003:145; Renard, 2002:262; Morgan, 2001:72).

In Hinduism, people overcome evil by their own individual, focused efforts along one of the four yogas. The key to successfully overcoming evil is found in first embracing a worldview that involves monism, and then by engaging in activities designed to train the self to intuitively recognize the delusion of self alongside the reality of Self. The responsibility for conquering the Hindu equivalent of evil lies with each individual.

Buddhism's Approach to Conquering Evil

Since Buddhism teaches that evil exists in the form of suffering, and since the cause and source of evil is clearly laid out, it is vital for Buddhism to offer a plan for the defeat, elimination (whole or partial), or subjugation of evil in human experience. The Third Noble Truth of Buddhism teaches that one can suppress suffering and that the possibility of *nirvana* exists. Nirvana is personal, inner peace that comes about when one is liberated from craving, attachment, and suffering (Das, 1998:84). Ancient Buddhist thought lays out the logical process for the cessation of craving and suffering (evil) in a logical fashion:

> But on the complete fading out and cessation of ignorance ceases *karma*;
> On the cessation of *karma* ceases consciousness;
> On the cessation of consciousness cease name and form;
> On the cessation of name and form cease the six organs of sense;
> On the cessation of the six organs of sense ceases contact;
> On the cessation of contact ceases sensation;
> On the cessation of sensation ceases desire;
> On the cessation of desire ceases attachment;
> On the cessation of attachment ceases existence;
> On the cessation of existence ceases birth;
> On the cessation of birth cease old age and death, lamentation, misery, grief, and despair. Thus does this entire aggregation of misery cease (Radhakrishnan & Moore, 1999:278-279).

The role of humanity in conquering evil is the only one that matters in Buddhist thinking. After all, there is no supreme God in Buddhism (Das, 1998:183, 244). For Buddhist branches that emphasize personal liberation (Therevada), the responsibility for conquering evil lies solely with each individual (Das, 1998:62-63). For Buddhist branches that emphasize widespread liberation (Mahayana) and a need to help all achieve enlightenment (Das, 1998:63), the vast majority of responsibility still lies with each individual. However, those who have already achieved enlightenment may offer some degree of help to those who have not yet achieved enlightenment. Buddhism refers to one of these individuals as a *bodhisattva* (Gethin, 1998:229; Das, 1998:143-144, 283). In some expressions of Buddhism, they can appear to be godlike. However, they are merely former humans who have achieved a new level of existence via enlightenment, and even then they remain far removed from the state of true and full enlightenment. As evidence of this, Gethin details the thirty-one realms of existence, from the lowest and least divine to the highest and most divine (Gethin, 1998:115-117). Of all the thirty-one realms of existence, human existence is fifth from the bottom (Gethin, 1998:116-177). The godlike states of existence are both slightly worse and slightly better than humans. Jealous and Hungry Gods occupy the two positions immediately below humans while the Yama Gods, the Thirty-Three Gods, and the Gods of the Four Kings occupy the positions immediately above humans (Gethin, 1998:116-177). There are twenty-three full realms of existence that are superior to these gods. Furthermore, the highest form of a god, the Great Brama, which is the closest equivalent to a theist's "God" (Gethin, 1998:114), occupies a position that is eighteen rungs from the top (Gethin, 1998:116-177). It is incorrect to equate even the Great Brama with an overarching, creating God in the way theism thinks of God (Gethin, 1998:114). While a bodhisattva may offer help to an individual, one must keep in mind that even gods are far from enlightenment, and the responsibility for overcoming evil lies with humans (Das, 1998:62-63).

The Fourth Noble Truth is a clear explanation of how evil is conquered. If one wishes to overcome evil, he or she will exercise strict adherence to the Eight-Fold Path (Radhakrishnan & Moore, 1999:278-279; Das, 1998:84, 88-89; Chodron, 1997:39). The first step in defeating evil (and the first step of the Eight-Fold Path) is for one to implement Right View. Correcting one's view to move away from ignorance and conform to the correct view of self is the starting point for conquering evil. Certainly, one must confront suffering and ignorance by first accepting that there is no perpetual self or other selves to blame. This approach begins to bring release to the sufferer (Chodron, 1997:39). The second step, Right Intentions, addresses the need to ensure that all of one's deeds proceed from selflessness. If one performs any deed for selfish gain or desire, then that reinforces attachment to self and works against enlightenment. Right Speech is the third step, and it is the first manifestation of Right View and Right Intentions into actions. Right Speech moves an individual toward goodness. It involves the words that one speaks and the motivation behind those words. Prayer is an interesting and important component of Right Speech. While it shares similarities in nomenclature and outward appearance with theistic prayer, the deep, underlying differences lead to a form of prayer that is distinct from theistic prayer, and one must take care to understand Buddhist prayer within its proper context. When a Buddhist prays, he or she is not praying to God; rather, the prayer is a personal affirmation of Right Intentions as expressed through Right Speech. It is spoken dharma and a vow to live properly. Prayer is directed within oneself as an internal affirmation as opposed to directing prayer outward as a petition to an external, supernatural being (Tanaka, 2002:87-89; Das, 1998:183). Right Action is the fourth step along the Eight-Fold Path. It consists of actions that display a higher level of wisdom and enlightenment by helping other people. This in turn helps oneself via the acquisition of good deeds and karma (Das, 1998:199). Right Livelihood is the fifth step along the Eight-Fold Path. It is a vocationally focused application of Right Action and dharma. It asks that one have a vocation (or make money) doing something that is consistent with dharma and does not harm others. Arms dealing, for example, would be a violation of Right Livelihood, but one's choice to be a compassionate veterinarian would qualify. Right Effort is the sixth step, and it means that someone who is seeking enlightenment and liberation from suffering must be diligent in pursuing the source of truth and freedom. Right Effort is more than mere intellectual assent to the doctrines of Buddhism; it involves a commitment to meditation, enthusiasm for it, and proper pursuit of spiritual discipline in general. Right Mindfulness is the seventh step, and while it is similar to Right View, it consists of living in a state of constant mindfulness of reality as it really is. It includes mindfulness regarding what one's proper place is in this reality. The final step along the Eight-Fold Path is Right Concentration. A person who has mastered this step is able to focus spirituality, energy, mental prowess, and attention to work for enlightenment (Das, 1998:334-335). In this final step along the Path, meditation comes in and takes center stage in how one conquers evil.

Regardless of the style of meditation used by various individuals, the goal is always the same: one must achieve enlightenment. External perceptions of reality are false, and the only perfect, continual truth lies strictly within one's own Buddha-nature. Truth and an accurate view of reality must be discovered and verified within oneself; only then can the false, external perceptions of reality be overcome (Goleman, 2003:96). If one is to escape the cycle of suffering induced by ignorance and craving, then one must have a clear understanding of how things really are. As a source of or a test for truth, all external experiences are intrinsically flawed. Therefore, one must use meditation to disconnect from ignorance and clear the mind from its afflicted state (Gethin, 1998:75). The *vipassana* meditation practiced in the Theravada tradition is an example of a particular technique that fulfills Right Meditation (Leve, 2002:850-852).

The practitioner of Buddhism who accepts the Four Noble Truths and who diligently follows the Eight-Fold Path through wisdom, ethics, and meditation training is on the correct path. Perfection of these three areas through his or her own efforts cleanses a Buddhist from ignorance, craving, attachment, aversion, and suffering. There is no divine aid in conquering evil; human adherence to the Path is how Buddhism conquers evil.

CHAPTER 12:

Creating a Universal Code of Classification for Systems of Evil

THE NEXT PORTION OF this study asks the question of how to create a universal code of classification and identification for evil. The previous chapter's identification of the major questions asked by each religious system affirmatively answers the antecedent question of whether or not it is possible to create a universal code of classification (hereafter referred to as "UCC"). The various and detailed answers allow for the possibility of a unified system of comparison to be developed, although it must be approached with diligence and detail, particularly with regard to creating or selecting a system that will properly contain and communicate the data.

The Challenge of Uniting Disparate Systems

There are vast differences among the religious systems under analysis in this study, not the least of which are contradictory worldviews that form the foundation of each faith. Besides properly handling the details of each faith, any proposed system must also be able to present these details side by side while acknowledging these fundamental differences. Therefore, the challenge in creating a UCC is threefold. First, the UCC must account for the differences in the religions, both major and minor. The UCC must be able to communicate the more obvious details as well as the subtle, implied differences due to disparate worldviews. Second, internal unity is a vital part of any UCC. That is, in spite of all the differences between religions, the UCC must identify topics of universal concern among the religions—even if the various faiths deal with these topics by different methods. For example, the subtleties of Hindu philosophy must be accurately represented side by side with specifics of Christian theology in a way that is common to both but faithful to each individually. Finally, the UCC must be an open system. It must be able to accept revision and addition as the result of future research.

The creation of the UCC uses Thomas Kuhn's approach to the scientific formulation of theories (1970). This approach involves three major steps: the identification of significant facts within the research data, the matching of these facts to a (newly) formulated theory, and the articulation of the theory (Kuhn, 1970:34). In the context of this work, the first step is to identify the significant facts that the UCC must address. In this study, identification of significant facts corresponds to the preceding chapters, which contain the bulk of the investigative research into identifying the core, common issues faced by each religion on the topic of evil and suffering. The second step of matching the discovered significant facts with a formulated theory takes place in this chapter by creating a UCC (this study's equivalent of Kuhn's formulated theory) to match the core issues (significant facts) discovered earlier. The final step takes place in the next chapters, at which point the details of the religions will be classified relative to each other in the newly developed UCC, and the sufficiency and consistency of the systems will be evaluated (matching Kuhn's final step of detailed articulation of the newly formulated theory).

Identification of Significant Facts

The research to this point indicates the existence of several significant facts (hereafter referred to as "SFs") with regard to the comparative study of evil. It is best to classify these SFs into two categories of data, *x* and *y*, where *x* is a specific question and *y* is a specific answer to *x*. Using this method, "SF*x*-*y*" represents this collection of data. In this context, *x* represents one of the four common questions about evil and suffering, such as asking if evil is real or illusory (question one from chapter 7, hence SF1-*y*). The *y* indicates the topical position taken by a specific religion (chapters 8-11), such as Judaism's view on a particular topic (SF*x*-J). Put together, SF1-J would be Judaism's position on the question of whether evil is real or illusory. The full list is as seen in figure 1 below:

SF1 The origin of evil

- ❏ SF1-J: Mostly human, some Divine
- ❏ SF1-C: Strictly human, excepting some evil spiritual activity
- ❏ SF1-I: Mostly human, some Divine
- ❏ SF1-H: Mostly Divine, but some human
- ❏ SF1-B: Strictly human

SF2 The reality of evil

- ❏ SF2-J: Real
- ❏ SF2-C: Real
- ❏ SF2-I: Real
- ❏ SF2-H: More illusion than real
- ❏ SF2-B: Real

SF3 The experiential value of evil

- ❏ SF3-J: No serious value, some mitigating outcomes
- ❏ SF3-C: Some value
- ❏ SF3-I: Some value

- ❑ SF3-H: No value
- ❑ SF3-B: No value

SF4 The defeat of evil

- ❑ SF4-J: Conquered mainly by humans, Divine has some role
- ❑ SF4-C: Conquered by the Divine
- ❑ SF4-I: Conquered mainly by humans, Divine has a small role
- ❑ SF4-H: Conquered by humans
- ❑ SF4-B: Conquered by humans

Figure 1: Full List of Significant Facts (SF*x-y*)

Formulation of a Universal Code of Classification

The identification and grouping of the SFs allows one to formulate a system that shows consistently how religions relate to each other while still accounting for their respective points of view (matching Kuhn's formulation of a theory). The presence of the common questions and their respective answers points toward a design for the UCC that emphasizes the relationship between the various answers to the common questions.

A purely textual representation (the list of SFs above) does not adequately provide the essentials of clarity, context, and consistency in a comparative study such as this. Key comparative data must accurately address those essentials in a way that is immediately clear and easy to understand (Wainer, 1984:137-147). Thus, a move away from pure text and toward a graphic representation of data is the next step. In the process of transferring raw data to a graphic display, one must be careful not to introduce unintentional inaccuracies or other concerns with regard to maintaining effective communication (Tukey, 1990:327-339). The challenge is to choose the best possible form of visual communication for this task, as the UCC will only be accurate and efficient if the visual decoding of the graphical representation is easy and effective (Cleveland and McGill, 1985:828).

Methodological and Practical Considerations in the Development of a Graphical Representation for the Classification of Significant Facts

In analyzing common mistakes made in creating graphical data constructs, Tukey identifies several key areas that one should consider. Many of these items deal with specific aspects of creating a system to aid one with effective visual decoding and mental processing of graphically represented data. They are universal with regard to method of display chosen (chalkboard, computer screen, or projection):

- Impact: the message delivered by the display must be vivid. The intention must be precise and clear to each individual viewer, even if the viewer disagrees with the message (Tukey, 1990:328, 336).
- Flow: the logical progression and analysis of the data points must come together with natural ease. One can address this by using common values, medians, and the relative distance between values, as well as by using identical, non-aligned scales in the case of multiple graphs (Tukey, 1990:328; Cleveland and McGill, 1985:830).
- Efficient transfer of recognition: given that there are many valid ways to present most sets of data (Kuhn, 1970:76), the UCC should use the fewest number of charts and objects in an effort to decrease visual clutter (Tukey, 1990:331).
- Context: the display method needs to be a contextual fit and clearly communicate the overall purpose of the data presentation (Tukey, 1990:332).

There are two additional areas of concern that are specific to the creation of this UCC. First, the UCC should be extensible. As this current study does not endeavor to include every religion, the UCC should be able to expand in order to support the inclusion of other religious views for future expansion. This also allows for different sects or denominational variations of religions (for example, if one wished to map all the different sects of Buddhism relative to each other). If the UCC is not extensible, then its usefulness is limited to the specific frame of this study. However, this study naturally invites further analysis (see final chapter).

Second, portability is a desirable component in the development of this UCC. The data presented in this study deals with religious concepts that are common to people from around the world, and people dialogue about these concepts in a wide variety of environments. Therefore, the UCC should make use of a display method that is usable in the widest variety of circumstances. Therefore, the UCC will not require specialized display equipment that would potentially limit the usefulness of this data to specific methods. For example, a UCC that requires an animated graphic on a computer screen would be limited to situations where a computer is involved. Ideally the UCC data should be presented and discussed free from equipment limitations in a variety of physical circumstances, such as in a book, in a paper, in an office, in a classroom, or during a casual conversation taking place in a neighborhood coffee shop.

Creating a Systematic Representation: Grouping Core Components and Developing a Universal Code of Classification

With all of the preceding concerns in mind, the best method to present the research data visually is to use two-axis scatter plots. A scatter plot is a two-dimensional graph that makes use of two perpendicular axes. This allows for spatial plotting of multiple data points, and these data points contain spatially significant meaning relative to the axes as well as to the other data points (see figure 2).

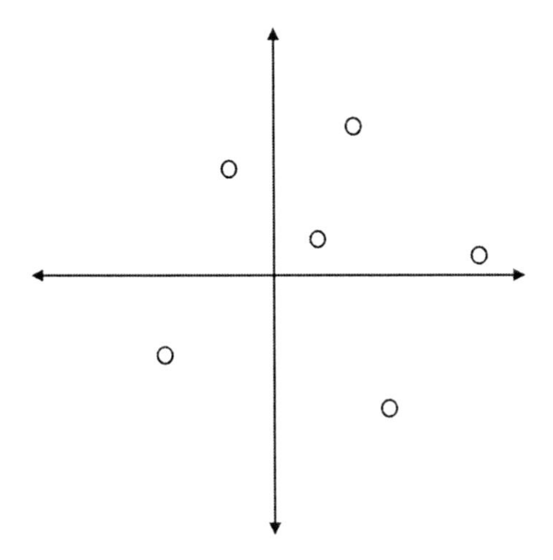

Figure 2: Example of a Scatter Plot with Multiple Data Points

Scatter plots allow one to present a variety of facts in an effective, visual manner that is immediately clear and easy to understand (Wainer, 1984:137-147). This also maintains clarity in terms of value, scale, and relative position (Tukey, 1990:328; Cleveland and McGill, 1985:830). To address a specific need of this study, scatter plots allow multiple data points to be plotted relative to common references. The axes of each chart represent the common questions asked (*x*). The visual data points represent the answers to each question (*y*), and they are plotted as relative to both the axes and each other.

The UCC will group the common questions (SF*x*) in two pairs (two axes per graph, one vertical and one horizontal as in figure 2, above). The greatest thematic similarities in the first part of data (SF*x*) determine the appropriate pairings for each graph. Therefore, the first pairing is the *origin of evil* matched with the *reality of evil*, and the second pairing is *the human experience of evil* together with *overcoming evil*. Therefore, the UCC labels the chart axes by SF*x* as in figures 3 and 4 (below). Arrows on the axes indicate an open-ended, and thereby extensible, UCC. Use of continuum-mapped positions (open-ended) allows for increased accuracy with regard to some specific issues (that do not handle absolute valuation gracefully) as well as allowing for future data points to be plotted beyond current maximums (extensibility). This allows for the addition of other religions, cults, or denominations that might otherwise go beyond the currently defined maximums inherent in a closed scale.

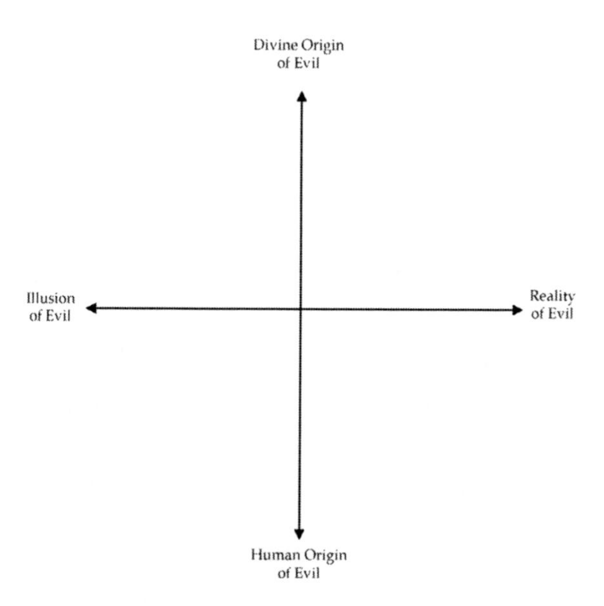

Figure 3: Charting Comparative Religious Concepts of Evil: the Nature of Evil

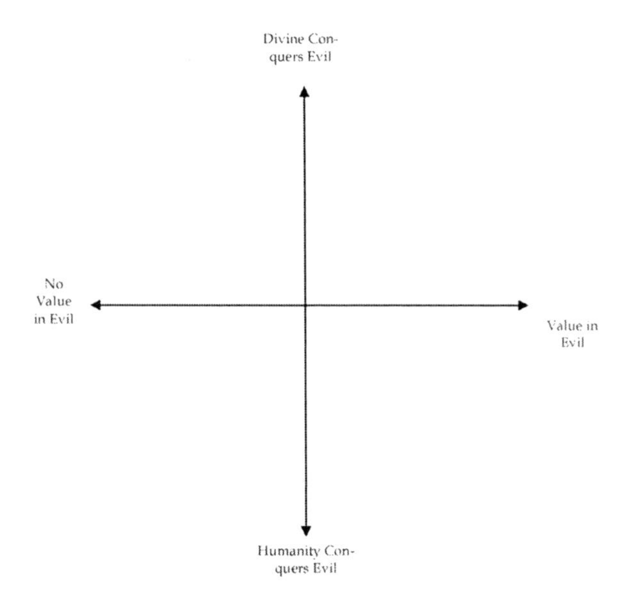

Figure 4: Charting Comparative Religious Concepts of Evil: the Experience of Evil

Having created the basis of the twin graphs by using the common questions as axes, the answers (*y*) are now ready for addition to the UCC. Use of similar scales to plot the answers addresses Cleveland and McGill's contention that proper visual data presentation makes use of common scales, and that it is preferable to use identical, but non-aligned, scales when multiple graphs are necessary (1985:830). Additionally, the use of this format satisfies many of the concerns with regard to visual decoding of data by enabling efficient impact, ease of flow, and the quick transfer and visual recognition of data points (Tukey, 1990:328, 338; Cleveland and McGill, 1985:830).

In order to address the issue of portability, one must take care in choosing what to use as basic symbols for plotting the data points for each religious position on the twin graphs. The UCC will avoid using color (which limits portability) and complex symbols (which slow down visual recognition of data) in favor of a simple and effective solution: the first initial of the appropriate religion will be used to plot the data points for each faith's respective positions (J, C, I, H, B). This continues to allow for quick, accurate communication of data in a way that is immediately clear and precise (Wainer, 1984:137-147; Tukey, 1990:328, 336). In addition, it will be easy to recognize the relative positions of the religions to each other and thus provide meaningful spatial-relation data at a glance (Tukey, 1990:328; Cleveland and McGill, 1985:830).

Nomenclature

One final step remains in the creation of the UCC. It is desirable to label a religion's full system of thought regarding evil in such a way as to identify it verbally or in written form. One should not have to list every SF*x*-*y* or use the twin graphs of the UCC every time one wants to communicate about a specific aspect of a particular religion's approach to theodicy. Use of proper nomenclature allows for precise communication, particularly when comparing various systems. Labelling the quadrants of each graph accomplishes this task (see figures 5 and 6, below).

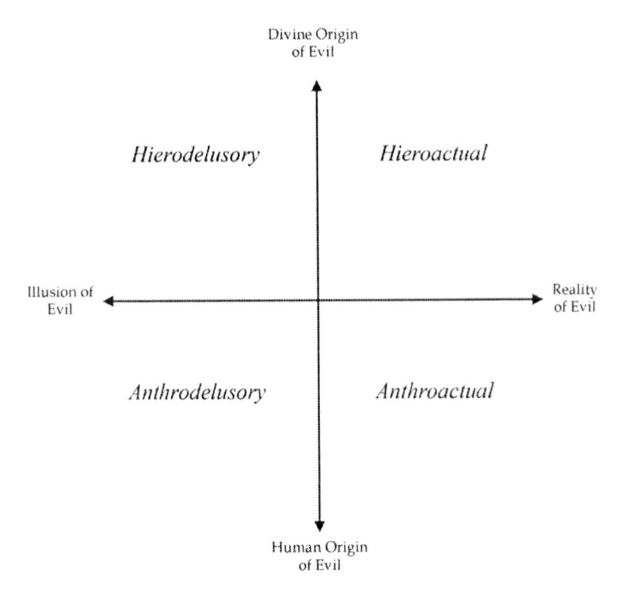

Figure 5: Nomenclature for the Nature of Evil

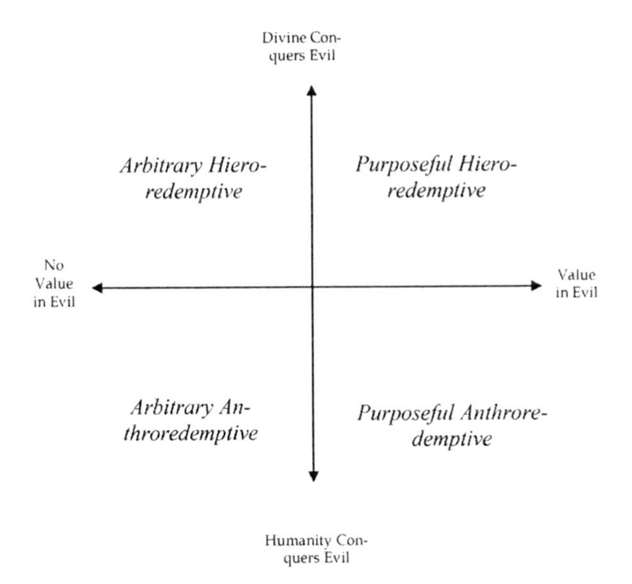

Figure 6: Nomenclature for the Experience of Evil

The UCC for the chart dealing with the nature of evil makes use of the prefixes *hiero* (Greek for "sacred," in the sense of the sacred-profane/divine-human contrast popularized by Eliade in his concept of hierophanies (1957)) and *anthro* (Greek for "human") when dealing with the origin of evil. The scale representing the reality or illusion of evil uses the words *delusory* and *actual* as suffixes. Hence, a system may be *hieroactual, hierodelusory, anthroactual,* or *anthrodelusory*. For the chart that details the experience of evil, there was no method that elegantly represented both the way evil is conquered and the value in the human experience of evil with the use of only a single word. Therefore, the proposed nomenclature uses two words in each quadrant. The issue of whether or not there is value in the human experience of evil uses the words *arbitrary* or *purposeful*. This is followed by the use of either *hieroredemptive* (the Divine conquers evil) or *anthroredemptive* (humanity conquers evil) for the topic of the conquering of evil. So, a particular quadrant is labelled as a combination of the two sub-labels, which results in: *arbitrary-hieroredemptive, arbitrary-anthroredemptive, purposeful-hieroredemptive,* or *purposeful-anthroredemptive*. This nomenclature allows for precise verbal or written reference to the overall system a faith embraces for its theodicy, and this study will use this nomenclature when engaged in systemic evaluation and critique (for example, when evaluating the overall propositions of a system that is *hieroactual*).

Summary

This study carefully applied the data gathered from the research in the preceding chapters in order to create the format of a UCC. It proposes the use of a graphical display method, and in an attempt to avoid common pitfalls and maximize communicative impact, pays close attention to display theory. Furthermore, the UCC maintains data portability as a way to maximize situational usefulness, and its design allows for future extensibility. The use of dual scatter plots allows for a precise, easily recognized representation of relative data points aligned by thematic commonality. With the form of the UCC settled, this study now moves to Kuhn's third and final step (articulation of theory). In doing so, the next chapter articulates the various data points (SF*x*-*y*) as part of the UCC.

CHAPTER 13:

Classifying the Major Religious Beliefs into a Universal Code of Classification

AT THIS POINT IN the process, the study will proceed with the first portion of Kuhn's final step (1970:34) by matching the articulation of facts (SF*x-y*) to the stated theory (the proposed UCC) by use of the dual scatter plot detailed in the previous chapter. The first step in this process is to plot a general position for every religion relative to each axis pairing, such as mapping a religion as *anthroactual* and *purposeful-hieroredemptive*. The second step is to adjust each individual religion's plot point within each quadrant to ensure positional accuracy relative to the plot points of the other religions (in order to address relative distance between values as per Tukey, 1990:328; Cleveland and McGill, 1985:830). This is critical for an accurate, comparative evaluation of religious thought concerning evil. For example, if two religions are both plotted as generally being *hierodelusory*, then proper positioning of each plot must also take into account how much emphasis "religion A" places on delusion versus how much emphasis "religion B" places on it. Religion B is plotted farther to the left (toward ever-increasing degrees of delusion) if religion B has a greater emphasis on the delusory nature of evil than religion A.

Classification of Tthe Concepts of Evil in the Major Religious Belief Systems According to the Universal Code of Classification

In taking the first step in appropriate plotting, one looks to the data provided in chapters 8 through 11. Using the dual scatter plots, the UCC now must assign general quadrant plots for each religious viewpoint (as seen in figure 7, below the lists).

The Nature of Evil

- ❑ Judaism is *anthroactual*: SF1-J is mostly human, some Divine; SF2-J is real.
- ❑ Christianity is *anthroactual*: SF1-C is strictly human, excepting some evil spiritual activity; SF2-C is real.
- ❑ Islam is *anthroactual*: SF1-I is mostly human, some Divine; SF2-I is real.
- ❑ Hinduism is *hierodelusory*: SF1-H is mostly Divine, but some human; SF2-H is more illusion than real.
- ❑ Buddhism is *anthroactual*: SF1-B is strictly human; SF2-B is real.

The Experience of Evil

- ❑ Judaism is *purposeful-anthroredemptive*: SF3-J has little value; SF4-J is conquered mainly by humans, some Divine.
- ❑ Christianity is *purposeful-hieroredemptive*: SF3-C has some value; SF4-C is conquered by the Divine.
- ❑ Islam is *purposeful-anthroredemptive*: SF3-I has some value; SF4-I is conquered mainly by humans, some Divine.
- ❑ Hinduism is *arbitrary-anthroredemptive*: SF3-H has no value; SF4-H is conquered by humans.
- ❑ Buddhism is *arbitrary-anthroredemptive*: SF3-B has no value; SF4-B is conquered by humans.

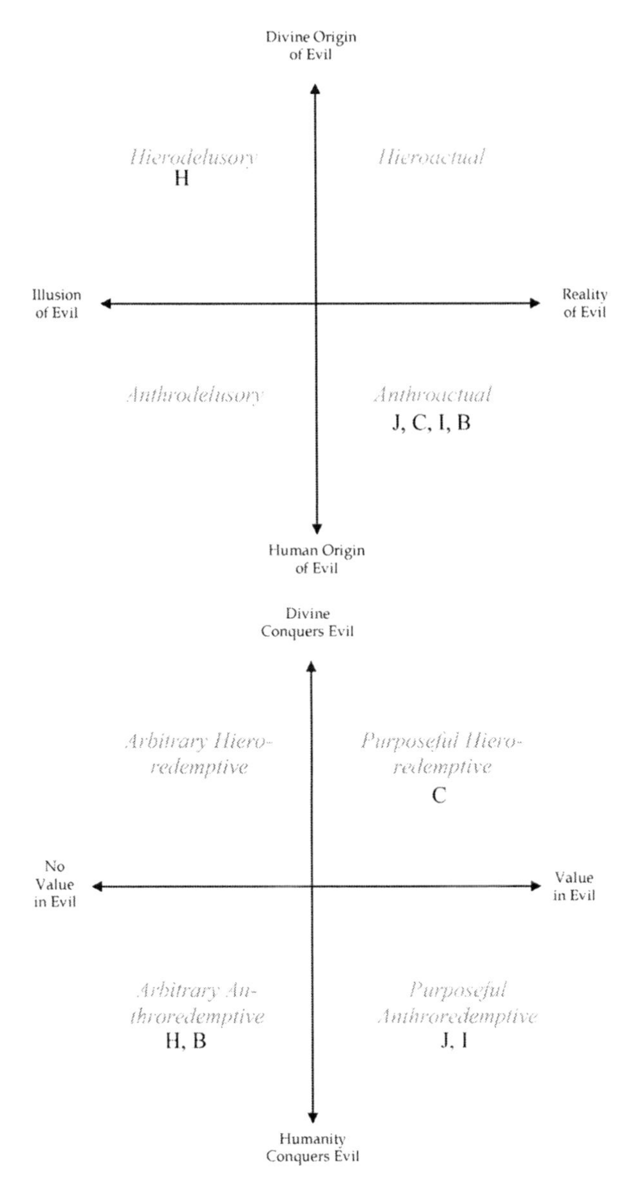

Figure 7: Initial, General Quadrant Plots

These placements are generally accurate with regard to the overall system used by each faith. However, with the current plotting in figure

7, there is no differentiation between religions based on variations or differences in emphasis between them. Therefore, a simple, general quadrant-based plot is not sufficient in order for the UCC to express the position held by each religion with full accuracy. Differences within a particular paradigm (i.e., differences between the four faiths that are *anthroactual*) necessitate representation by individual positional accuracy relative to the core issues (the topical axes). Also, one must account for positional accuracy relative to other religions that are part of the same paradigm (the other plots in the same quadrant). If the UCC does not do this, then the plotting fails to provide visual comparison of significant facts by use of common values, medians, and the relative distance between values (Tukey, 1990:328). Therefore, the next step is to analyze and compare the religious systems with each other along common, topical axes, and then to plot their appropriate, relative positions.

Plotting the Reality of Evil

To say that evil in Hinduism is more illusion than real is accurate, but one also needs to acknowledge that there is an experiential component to evil even in Hinduism. Because of this, one should not claim totality of illusion when plotting a place for Hinduism. To approximate an answer as to how much evil is real as opposed to how much it is unreal, Hinduism should occupy a place that is past the midpoint on the side of illusion, but not so far past the midpoint as to imply complete illusion. However, it should be close to the far edge, as the major thrust of Hindu scriptures and practices is in line with the illusory nature of evil. When this is considered, the proper plot for the Hindu reality of evil is just short of the edge of illusion on the chart.

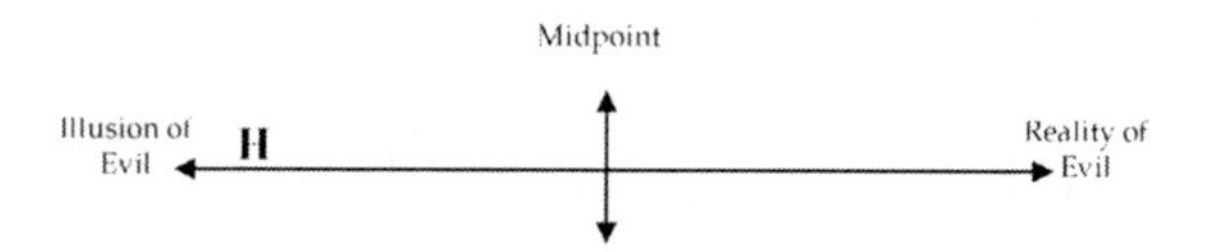

Figure 8: Plotting the Reality of Evil, Step 1

The theistic religions are very similar to each other and should occupy the same position. Evil is real for theistic faiths. The appropriate, specific position that the theistic faiths should occupy is at the edge of the scale indicating reality (as there is no significant difference in how real evil is among those religions).

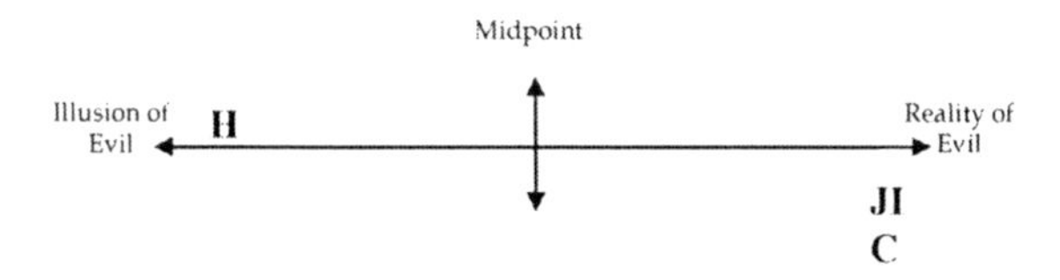

Figure 9: Plotting the Reality of Evil, Step 2

The proper plot for the idea of evil in Buddhism is on the side of reality. However, theistic faiths teach the full reality of the self and the full reality of suffering, while Buddhism teaches the doctrine of no-self (Das, 1998:118-119; Gethin, 1998:138-139; Goleman, 2003:79). This is a move away from the reality of the theistic faiths and toward the Hindu position. Since suffering is considered real (Gethin, 1998:59-60), and since Buddhist adherents ought to defeat it (Gethin, 1998:74, Das, 1998:199), evil is plotted as real, but its plot is lowered to a degree of reality less than that of the theistic faiths in order to represent the incremental move away from theism's position and toward Hinduism's view.

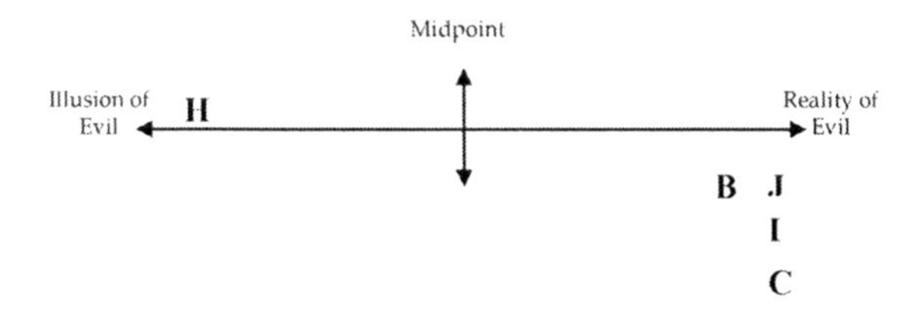

Figure 10: Plotting the Reality of Evil, Final

Plotting the Origin of Evil

Hinduism is the only religion in this study that places the bulk of the origin of evil on the side of the divine. While Hinduism is the only religion with a plot beyond the median line on the side of the divine origin of evil, one should be careful to plot the lone point in such manner as to represent the approximate extent to which the origin of evil lies with the divine. Since Hinduism still places some degree of responsibility for the origin of evil with humanity, though not much, one should plot it approximately one-third past the median along the divine side of the scale. This indicates that the Divine is primarily responsible for evil, while being careful not to discount a human role, and to the uninitiated viewer this will clearly indicate the role of the Divine while not obfuscating the role of humanity.

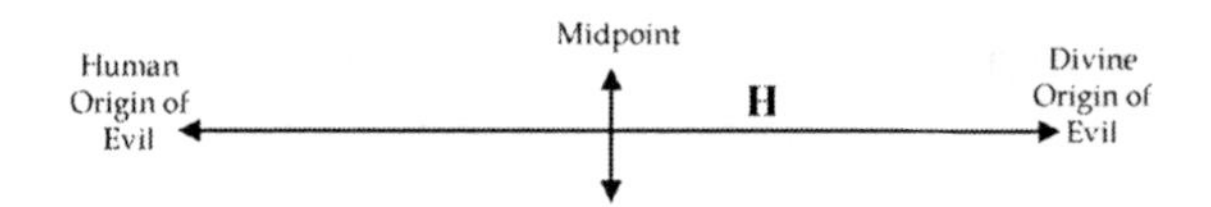

Figure 11: Plotting the Origin of Evil, Step 1

All of the remaining religions give greater weight to the human origin of evil, and they all occupy various positions on that side of the chart. Buddhism and Christianity both give a great amount of importance to a human origin. For the sake of comparison, it is worth noting that Christian theodicy deals with this issue in explicit detail. On the other hand, Buddhism does not explicitly explain this issue in its handling of the topic; rather, it is more implicit in its underlying philosophy. Buddhism's reluctance to acknowledge true human existence, the doctrine of no self (Das, 1998:118-119; Gethin, 1998:138-139; Goleman, 2003:79), does not absolve humanity from its role in the origin of suffering. Christianity, which explicitly endorses actual human existence and the responsibility of humans for evil, also acknowledges a role played by Satan and demons. Mainstream Buddhism does not have a similar teaching, and there is no one else to share the blame for the origin of evil. With that in mind, both Christianity and Buddhism should be plotted near the far edge of having a human origin, but Buddhism should be plotted farther along the axis toward human origin with Christianity plotted near Buddhism, but just a bit closer to the median in order to account for the supernatural role of Satan and demons.

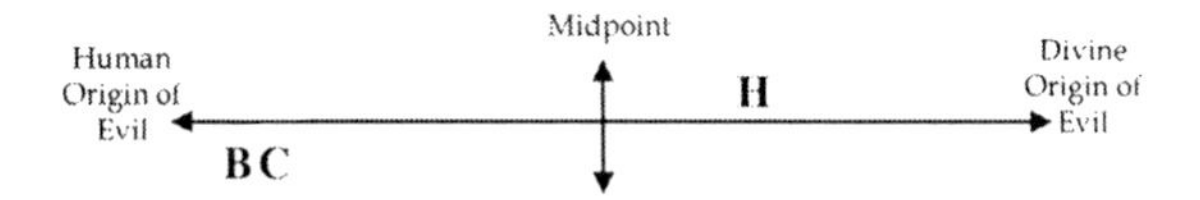

Figure 12: Plotting the Origin of Evil, Step 2

Both Islam and Judaism also give greater weight to the human origin of evil than to the Divine, but because of the teachings of the bad or evil impulse, they are significantly different from Buddhism and Christianity. Use of plots that are much closer to the median will adequately communicate their differences, although they are still on the side of a human origin. Judaism's theological conundrum introduced by the God-created evil impulse necessitates placement close to the median (Satlow, 2003:216), but it is still on the side of human origin. Islam's bad impulse is similar to the evil impulse, but its role is not as significant as it is in Judaism. In Islamic theology, the bad influence is more of a mere mechanism than a metaphysically significant force. Additionally, Judaism's evil impulse is far stronger than Islam's bad impulse. Furthermore, Judaism fully expects people to succumb to the evil impulse and sin, though they ought not to (Steinberg, 1985:89; Heschel, 1976:393; Ariel, 1995:91), but Islam fully expects a good Muslim to overcome the bad impulse and to live perfectly (Ali, 1990:144). Therefore, the plot for Islam should be farther beyond Judaism's plot in the direction of a more human origin, but it should still be closer to Judaism than to Christianity. The appropriate plot point for Judaism, while still on the side of a human origin, is closer to the median than to any of the other faiths.

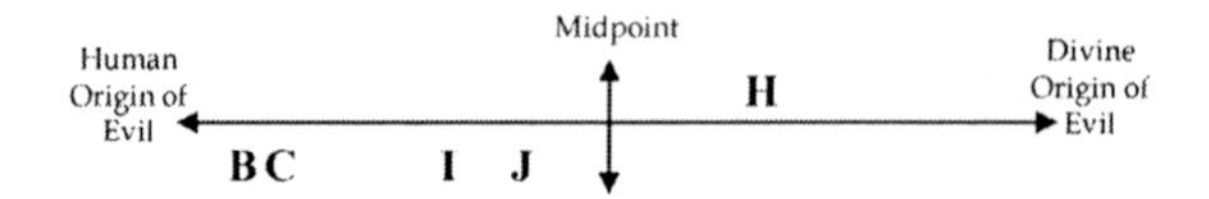

Figure 13: Plotting the Origin of Evil, Final

Plotting Human Value in the Experience of Evil

In Buddhism and Hinduism, the human experience of evil produces little or no value. In both of these religions, the perception or experience of evil serves only to enforce improper perspectives and perpetuate an undesirable (and incorrectly perceived) sense of self. The proper plot for Hinduism is at the far edge of proving no value because of this view. With regard to Buddhism's position, it is possible (though perhaps unlikely) for extreme attachments and aversions to cause significant enough pain to cause one to seek relief by decreasing the attachments and aversions. Therefore, the proper plot for Buddhism is a degree closer to the median than Hinduism. However, it should still reside near to the far edge so as not to indicate any significant value.

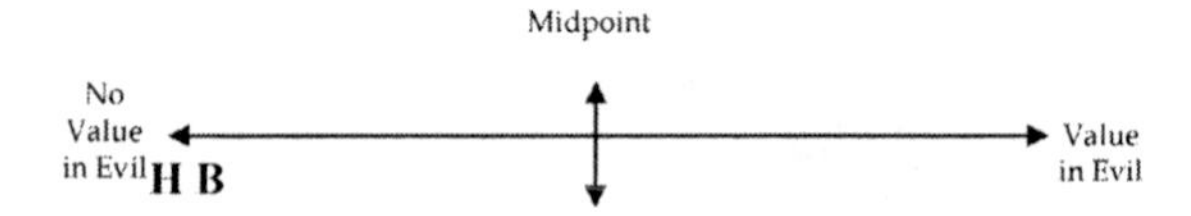

Figure 14: Plotting Value in the Human Experience of Evil, Step 1

Judaism, Christianity, and Islam all ascribe varying degrees of value to the human experience of evil. However, none of their respective theological positions embrace a doctrine that denotes the exact same level of value. Because of these differences, relative plotting is required in order to differentiate accurately between them. Judaism offers little in the way of value in the experience itself but does allow for some development of positive characteristics (although not because of God determining that the positive characteristics must develop). Most of the value Judaism accords to these situations comes from actions one may take in the face of evil (such as choosing to resist it), and therefore the value is not in the experience itself. Islam differentiates between the evil experiences that result from free-will choices to ignore divine revelation and the evil experiences that God sends to test and improve believers. In the case of evil experiences originating in one's free-will choices, there is no value of note. However, in the case of evil experiences resulting from deliberate testing, there is value in that these experiences can move a believer toward perfection. Christianity goes even further by claiming that God deliberately uses experiences of evil to increase desirable attributes. This exceeds the value offered by the previous two religions in two ways. First, this value is present in all cases of evil and it does not appear to be limited to specific circumstances (James 1:2-4). Second, the promise of God in the Christian scriptures implies divine determinism in making good come out of all things (even non-deterministic evils) as opposed to an arbitrary chance that good may ensue (Romans 8:28). Note that this only applies as a reaction to evil and in no way implies divine determinism in the origin of evil. When it comes to plotting the positions relative to each religion, Judaism should be placed just barely on the side of providing some value, with Islam offering a bit more, and with Christianity offering more than Islam. Christianity does promise some value in all cases, but the value it offers is not overwhelming. Therefore, the proper plot for Christianity in this context is halfway between the median and the far edge. That leaves Islam's plot, which should be placed somewhere between the points for Judaism and Christianity. Given its split between the two scenarios of human free will and divinely originated tests, and given its split between positions that are similar to both Judaism and Christianity, it is appropriate to plot its position halfway between the positions of those two faiths.

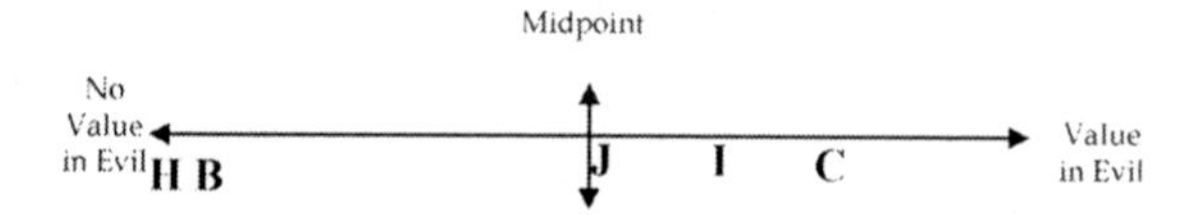

Figure 15: Plotting Value in the Human Experience of Evil, Final

Conquering Evil

Christianity is alone in claiming that evil is ultimately conquered entirely by the Divine. As God alone conquers evil in Christianity, the proper plot is at the farthest point away from the median at the far edge.

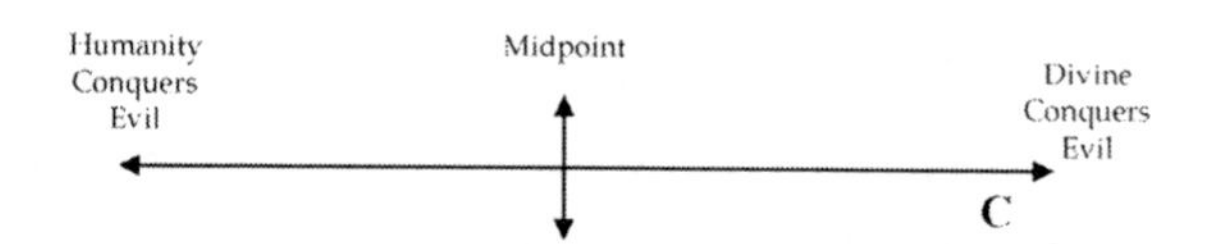

Figure 16: Plotting the Conquering of Evil, Step 1

The remaining faiths all claim varying degrees of human responsibility for ultimately conquering evil (either purely human or a mix of Divine and human with a greater portion of the responsibility being human). Hinduism and Buddhism are very similar in their respective approaches to conquering evil as they both give the responsibility for the defeat of evil almost entirely to humanity. The plots for both Hinduism and Buddhism belong at the same position at the far edge of human responsibility.

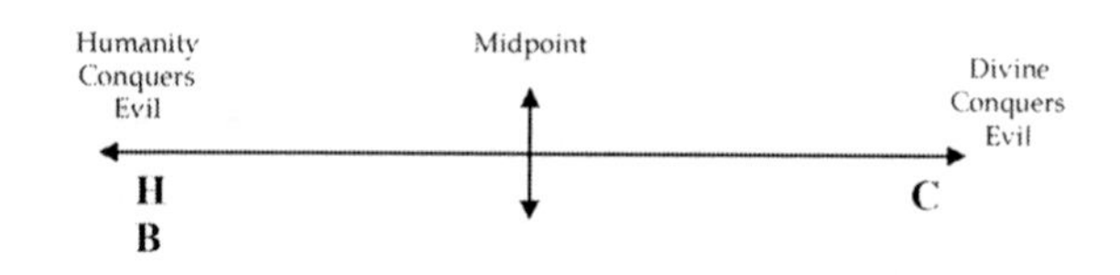

Figure 17: Plotting the Conquering of Evil, Step 2

Judaism and Islam teach a shared responsibility for conquering evil. Both claim that the majority of responsibility is on humans, and so at a basic level their points should be plotted somewhere on the human side along with Buddhism and Hinduism. However, while they both agree that the majority of responsibility is on humanity, they differ when it comes to precisely how much responsibility lies with humanity and how much lies with God. Judaism provides a greater emphasis on the eschatological portion of the solution that is in God's hands than Islam does, although it is still far less than the emphasis used by Christianity. In addition, Islam outdoes Judaism in putting the burden on humanity by virtue of its expectation that people should be able to live perfectly (Ali, 1990:144). Going even further, the intense societal and governmental regulations that are an intrinsic part of Islam further emphasize the human role (Nasr, 2003:110; Moosa, 2000-2001:187; Moaddel, 2002:379; Houben, 2003:149). With these data points in mind, Judaism should be plotted far enough past the median to communicate the emphasis on the role of humanity, but not so far past as to improperly diminish the role of the Divine in an eschatological solution. Islam should go ever farther beyond Judaism, and its final position is equidistant between the position shared by the non-theistic faiths and the position occupied by Judaism.

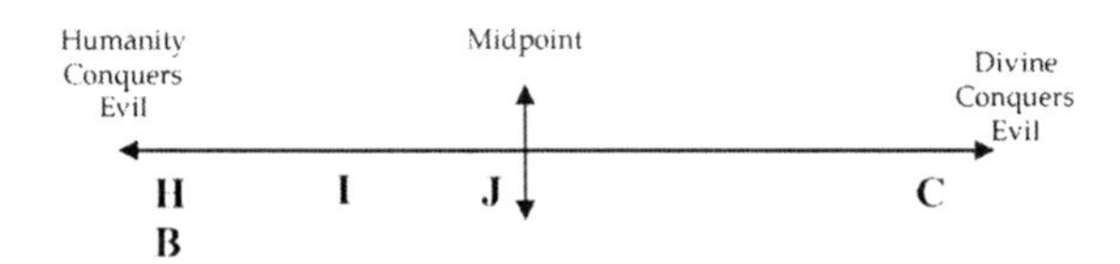

Figure 18: Plotting the Conquering of Evil, Final

Final Plots

Use of the UCC enables visual comparison between each specific religion and the four axes, and this study proposes plot points for each of their respective positions regarding evil. Analysis of the differences between religious systems that share similar paradigms has allowed for classification that is accurate in relation to the four main questions asked by each religion regarding evil (the four axes), and it is also accurate with regard to relative positions between religions. The final plotting of the systems is in figures 19 and 20.

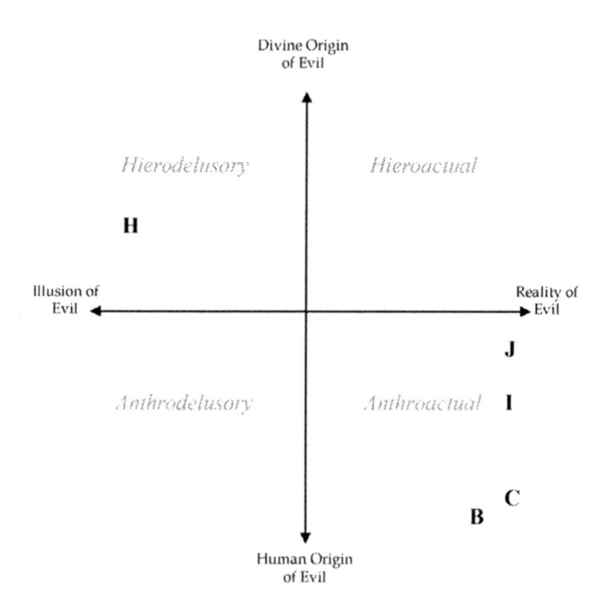

Figure 19: The Nature of Evil, Final

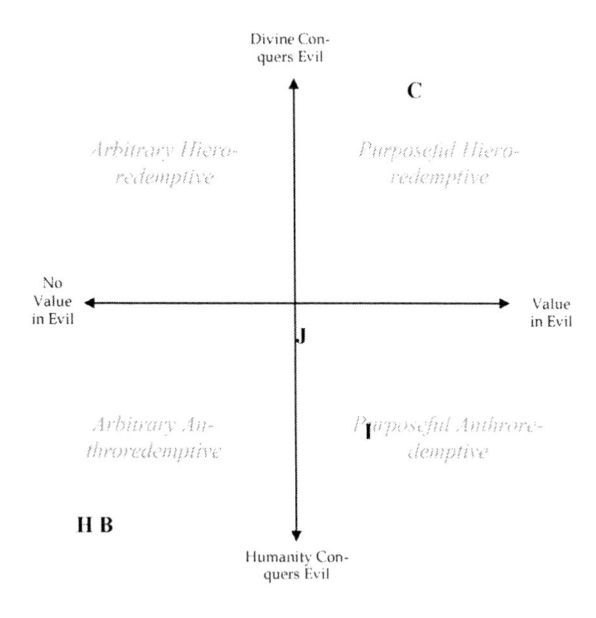

Figure 20: The Experience of Evil, Final

Effective Dialogue about Religious Concepts of Evil and Suffering Using the UCC

As discussed in the introductory chapter, many of the discussions between religious systems about evil and suffering focus on specific perspectives or on a single discipline. Because of deep and perhaps subtle differences, oftentimes the communication is mismatched and ineffective (recall the example of prayers in Buddhism and Christianity that appear similar in form but are extremely disparate). The UCC enables interfaith dialogue on the topic of evil and suffering in a way that makes use of the common denominators found in each faith (the four main questions about evil). This allows for *systemic* dialogue.

For example, many conversations between a Buddhist and a Christian about the value and role of prayer with regard to suffering might rely on each individual's religious presuppositions that do not apply to the other person's religion. Often a conversation would focus on the role of a particular, such as prayer. However, in this example of focusing on the particular of prayer, it is possible that no accurate, meaningful engagement would occur since the underlying belief systems are not compatible. Each participant may be unaware of the underlying disparities. Further, each participant may be unaware of how those disparities affect particular issues of each faith, such as the form and function of prayer. Prayer in Christianity relies on a real God to intervene in human lives (Grudem, 1994:376-392), but prayer in Buddhism relies on oneself to solve the problem and save oneself (Das, 1998:58, 183). Debating the particulars of prayer does not resolve anything since the topic has a different systemic root: regardless of prayer taking place, does God solve problems such as this, or do humans solve them?

Engaging in a systemically aware dialogue can be a key aid for interfaith interactions. If a Christian missionary wishes to argue effectively for the supremacy of Christ's sacrifice on the cross with a Hindu devotee, the first thing that must take place is a systemic conversion. For a conversion to be successful, the Hindu devotee must move away from the Hindu belief in a system that teaches that humanity saves itself via its actions, the four yogas. Rather, he or she must embrace a system that teaches that humanity is incapable of saving itself and that God must intervene to save humankind. A systemically aware dialogue is desirable when discussing theodicies that do not share underlying theological systems.

Particulars as Having Significance with a Systemic Paradigm

When theodicies share a general system (such as Buddhism, Islam, Judaism, and Christianity all being *anthroactual*), then the role of specific details can be an appropriate focal point for interfaith dialogue. For example, sin may be a difficult topic when engaged in interfaith dialogue between Hinduism and Christianity because of vast differences in their underlying theologies. However, discussing sin and its role in the origin of evil may be far easier as part of the interfaith dialogue held among the theistic faiths. The particular topic of the impact of sin (fallen nature versus neutral nature or good nature) is meaningful with regard to the topic of evil when the faiths use the same system. Likewise, the role of Jesus is logically and radically different in a *hieroredemptive* system as opposed to *anthroredemptive* systems, and any discussion of the particular topic of Jesus as manifestation, *bodhisattva*, rabbi, prophet, or God incarnate must first acknowledge the systemic differences (or similarities) between religions.

Summary

This study's application of the SF*x-y* in the proposed UCC established a framework for understanding various theodicies. Use of the UCC addressed several concerns with regard to developing a code of classification: clarity and ease (Wainer, 1984:137-147), impact (Tukey, 1990:328, 336), flow (Tukey, 1990:328; Cleveland and McGill, 1985:830), transfer of recognition (Tukey, 1990:331), and context (Tukey, 1990:332), along with the author's addition of portability and extensibility. This also satisfies Kuhn's third and final step (1970:34), which is matching the facts to an articulated theory.

This UCC enables effective interfaith dialogue by making use of thematic and theological common denominators in a way that crosses over cultural and religious presuppositions. This enables accurate, systemic interaction when engaged in interfaith dialogue on evil and suffering. The UCC also frames discussion about the particulars of the faiths in such manner as to allow appropriate comparisons or contrasts within a common context that preserves the individuality of each faith while maintaining a common, guiding construct.

The UCC introduces the possibility of sixteen paradigms, listed in figure 21 below. An individual's use of the UCC as proposed in the previous two chapters creates an opportunity for balanced and evenhanded interfaith dialogue on the topic of evil and suffering. Note that most of the potential paradigms defined by the UCC are unused by the religions in this study; however, those paradigms remain important as they may be appropriate for the many religious views that are not represented here. The religions in this study fall on both sides of the four main topics regarding evil (evil is: real or illusion, from God or humans, meaningful or not, and primarily conquered by God or humans). In figure 21, when a participating religion is described by a specific paradigm, it is marked with bold type. For example, in the context of the UCC, Hinduism uses a *hierodelusory/arbitrary-hieroredemptive* paradigm for evil, and this creates a point of communication for interfaith dialogue regarding evil and suffering. In order for a Christian adherent to participate accurately and fairly in this dialogue, he or she must be familiar with how Christianity's paradigm for evil represents its positions within the context of the UCC as well as how that position relates to the others.

Hierodelusory/arbitrary-hieroredemptive (Hinduism)
Hierodelusory/arbitrary-anthroredemptive (unused in this study)
Hierodelusory/purposeful-hieroredemptive (unused in this study)
Hierodelusory/purposeful-anthroredemptive (unused in this study)
Hieroactual/arbitrary-hieroredemptive (unused in this study)
Hieroactual/arbitrary-anthroredemptive (unused in this study)
Hieroactual/purposeful-hieroredemptive (unused in this study)
Hieroactual/purposeful-anthroredemptive (unused in this study)
Anthrodelusory/arbitrary-hieroredemptive (unused in this study)
Anthrodelusory/arbitrary-anthroredemptive (unused in this study)
Anthrodelusory/purposeful-hieroredemptive (unused in this study)
Anthrodelusory/purposeful-anthroredemptive (unused in this study)
Anthroactual/arbitrary-hieroredemptive (unused in this study)
Anthroactual/arbitrary-anthroredemptive (Buddhism)
Anthroactual/purposeful-hieroredemptive (Christianity)
Anthroactual/purposeful-anthroredemptive (Judaism and Islam)

Figure 21: Paradigms for Evil

In order for an individual to be effective in advocating any particular paradigm during the course of interfaith dialogue, participants must view the paradigm as generally consistent and able to offer a sufficient (not necessarily superior) explanation or solution for the problem of evil. Acknowledging a paradigm as sufficient does not mean that everyone involved in the dialogue has to agree with the methods, conclusions, or particulars of the particular paradigm. Rather, sufficiency indicates that a paradigm is workable and acceptable, perhaps one of several workable and acceptable paradigms. By contrast, if a particular paradigm is self-contradictory or fallacious, then it does not offer a sufficient approach to the topic. Therefore, it is necessary to examine the sufficiency of Christian theodicy's paradigm through an evaluation of logical, historical, theological, and experiential consistency.

CHAPTER 14:

The Logical Consistency of the Christian Paradigm for Evil

WHEN EXAMINING THE LOGICAL consistency of any paradigm, one looks for strengths in terms of internal consistencies and logical stability, or one looks for weaknesses in terms of logical inconsistencies or the presence of fallacies. When specifically looking at the logical consistency of the Christian paradigm for evil (as defined by the four corresponding areas of the UCC), one begins with Christianity's claim that evil is more real than illusion. The first challenge is to address an apparent logical inconsistency (as presented by some atheistic thinkers) in theistic theodicies regarding the existence and origin of evil compared to the nature of God: if there is an all-good, all-powerful God, and if evil exists, then God is not all-powerful or all-good (Ingersoll, 2000:80-82; Russell, 2000:92-93). This argument is designed either to destroy the theistic concept of God or the concept of evil as a reality. However, this attempt to prove that the Christian view is logically inconsistent suffers from *cum hoc* and *bifurcation* fallacies.

A cum hoc fallacy erroneously concludes a causal relationship when instead there is merely a correlative aspect. For example, several Celtic burial mounds at Hohenasperg, near Stuttgart, Germany, remain unexcavated because of modern buildings and businesses that an excavation effort would disturb (Ellis, 1998:47). In the years since the discovery of the presence of many burial mounds (and the lack of excavation), the number of educational departments offered by the Universität Stuttgart has decreased from a high of eighteen to fourteen in 1988, and down to a low of ten in 2003 (Engler, 2009). Therefore, the decrease in the number of educational departments is due to the lack of investigation and excavation of the burial mounds. This cum hoc fallacy notes the correlation between the two initial statements (the time frame of the discovery and the start of the decline in the number of departments), but it fallaciously assumes causality.

A bifurcation fallacy presents a false dilemma by restricting the number of choices to less than there ought to be (often two choices, an either-or dilemma). For example, one may present a bifurcation fallacy saying that a person must either be "for" or "against" expansion of the World Heritage Museum in Hallstatt, Austria. This is a false dilemma as it excludes the options of true neutrality, ignorance, or indifference. One can further amplify this fallacy by presenting one of the two choices as clearly (and perhaps deceptively) undesirable, thus falsely leading one toward the single, desired choice. Using the same example, one could say that the "for the expansion" option would demolish a significant portion of the local business district, which sounds bad and might lead people to choose the "against" option. However, in a tiny village such as Hallstatt, this may only involve expanding into an unused, open area that currently contains only a single tree and a large unoccupied space of cobblestones. This bifurcation fallacy is deceptive and leads people to false view of reality.

The argument that if evil exists, then God must have created it (Ingersoll, 2000:80-82; Russell, 2000:92-93) fallaciously assumes causation (cum hoc). While Judaism and Islam stumble a little bit on this point because of their doctrines of the evil and bad impulses,

Christianity deftly avoids this philosophical pothole by defining evil as a privation (Fernandes, 2002a:123-124; Geisler, 2002:46-47; Hines, 2003:325). This still allows for an all-good, all-powerful God alongside the existence of an actual evil that He did not create. Evil can exist as a privation, which is uncreated. As previously demonstrated, privations are real. Therefore, this argument against the reality of evil is a cum hoc fallacy.

Further, the continuing existence of evil does not necessitate a sadistic God who does not want to or is not able to conquer evil. To suggest otherwise is a bifurcation fallacy as other options are available. God can desire to conquer evil and not have done it yet as He will conquer evil *in the fullness of His perfect timing.* Finite minds cannot determine the perfect time and circumstances for evil's elimination; only God can do that, which He did via the Cross (Wright, 2006:88; 94, 136-137; Boyd, 2003:91, 118; Grudem, 1994:614-615; Henry, 1999:304; Erickson, 1998:475). It is entirely possible that the best possible world, with the greatest amount of good set against the absence of evil, can only be achieved through evil's defeat at a future point in time that can only be known to the infinite, sovereign God (Geisler and Feinberg, 1987:334).

Another attack on the reality of evil describes it as an illusion that is rooted in one's specific perspective and experience. In *Beyond Good and Evil,* Nietzsche's approach to this topic described evil as a matter of perspective and power. In this view, evil is an illusion as opposed to a metaphysical reality (1998:153-156). This is a view that Shelly echoes (2000:74-75). Their approach allows for complete subjectivity in evaluating what is evil, and this essentially renders the differentiation between good and evil meaningless in its absolute relativity. Evil only exists as a perception coming from the weaker person who is experiencing the power of the greater person. There is no real evil. However, people generally view something like the rape of a child as morally evil and not a matter of perspective; it seems to be a part of natural moral law.

It is inconsistent to embrace these views of Nietzsche and Shelly while simultaneously outlawing rape and comforting victims. If one truly believes that evil is purely subjective and relative, then one would live for oneself only, with no apparent regard to others, social norms, or laws; only one's personal pursuit of gratification would matter. Yet, according to the United Kingdom's Mental Health Act 1983, this would be a psychopathic disorder (United Kingdom, 1983). This shows that treating evil purely as a matter of perspective and position is inconsistent with human experience and moral certainty (Geisler and Brooks, 1990:140).

Naturalists, such as Shermer, embrace a view that disposes of all metaphysical concepts of good and evil while embracing the concepts of natural good and evil. In this view, metaphysical evil is illusion, but natural evil is reality. Shermer bases the evaluation of good on progress toward human evolution and the preservation of the human species and society. He defines evil as hindrance of the same (2004). The atheistic, naturalist view that evil is a metaphysical non-reality posits as its highest good the superiority of the human species and the moral necessity of its continued advancement. Yet this view confers supreme value on the human animal without using a higher, external, and objective measure. In this approach, humans are the supreme value because they say they are, and (from the human perspective) because they think they are the ascendant species. This valuation begs the question. In order to ascribe higher value to the human animal than to any other form of life (for example, the preservation and evolution of *acanthurus sohal* over that of *Homo sapiens*), then one must accept the existence of an even higher order that is able to make that determination. Eliade's concept of the value of hierophanies (the manifestation of the sacred providing an ontological foundation and point of reference for the profane) illustrates this concept well (Eliade, 1957:21-23). However, if one acknowledges something that is able to ascribe value to humanity (i.e., God or anything supernatural), then both the nonexistence of metaphysical valuation and the absolute supremacy of humanity are invalidated.

Religions based on pantheism or various expressions of monism often teach an illusory nature of evil. If all of perceived existence is actually part of the same, unified reality, then there cannot be any true differentiation (such as good and evil). Pure unity, as expressed in the singular, monistic existence, has no differentiation, and any perception to the contrary is delusory. This view is evident in several Hindu writings, including Krishna's famous speech to Arjuna (Bhagavad Gita 9.1-34). Christian Science, a Westernized form of Hindu philosophy, also proposes that evil is an illusion. It is explicit in its teaching of a singular Mind (monistic existence). Therefore, all the things that people perceive to be evil are actually non-differentiated parts of the singular Mind. This means that there is no actual, true differentiation, and perceptions of suffering and evil are illusions that will cease to plague a person when he or she recognizes it to be truly non-existent (Eustace, 1999:712-722). However, these views offer an unsatisfying and inconsistent explanation for evil. Adherents have no guarantee for the defeat of evil, and there is no value in the human experience of an illusion. Yet, despite "knowing" the illusory nature of evil and self, the suffering of a person who is slowly tortured to death is persistent and seems real. This violates correspondence theory. Correspondence theory has several variations, but it is a long-standing concept that, in its basic form, states that something is true if and only if it corresponds to reality (David, 2009; Dowden & Swartz, 2004). The proposition that all suffering and evil is illusion simply does not correspond in any way to the facts of the universal reaction of people to the suffering of torture or the experience of burning alive. By contrast, Christianity's acknowledgment of the reality of evil is logically consistent with regard to correspondence theory. Embracing the reality of evil is consistent with the history of human behavior, social controls, and governmental laws, all of which are based on objective moral laws, in contrast to the opposing view which would have no ability to logically posit objective moral values (Fernandes, 2009:93). The attacks on the reality of evil are inadequate in attempting to dismiss it as an illusion.

If the Christian view of the origin of evil is to be logically consistent, one must reconcile aspects of its existence with both divine characteristics and the expectation placed on humanity (in terms of both religious and social boundaries and burdens). It appears easy to claim that evil comes from the same source that created everything else, but for faiths that proclaim the goodness of God, there is a struggle to reconcile the origin of evil with God's creation of it (Satlow, 2003:216). While none of the religions in this study intentionally endorse a doctrine of divine sadism, nonetheless, it seems inconsistent to deny a doctrine of at least limited divine sadism if a particular doctrine teaches that some evil comes from God. A move toward a utilitarian justification (the ends justify the means) is an option for religions in this undesirable position. However, utilitarianism has several well-known weaknesses of its own (Geisler and Feinberg, 1987:393-395). A God who settles for intentionally creating evil as part of a utilitarian grand plan could indeed be seen as partially sadistic; alternatively, God may wish to have a world free from evil, but He may be too weak to be all-good in practice (Geisler and Corduan, 2003:298-300). This hearkens back to and seems to justify the attacks made by Ingersoll and Russell (Ingersoll, 2000:80-82; Russell, 2000:92-93). Christianity avoids these logical problems by placing the origin of evil with humanity. Evil entered creation when Adam fell, despite Satan's previously existing rebellion against God. This is the point where human nature became corrupt and nature began to suffer because of the curse. Further, if evil even partially originates from the Divine, then one may question the duty of an individual or society to resist evil. It is contradictory to posit a divine power that calls all of creation "good" or "very good" (Genesis 1:10-31) and then causes evil or creates an evil impulse. With regard to the duty of the individual to avoid temptation, the Christian paradigm offers logical consistency in this area as people cannot claim that God forced or influenced them to choose evil. "Let no one say when he is tempted, 'I am being tempted by God'; for God cannot be tempted by evil, and He Himself does not tempt anyone" (James 1:13). People may only claim that they chose to do evil. This also creates the opportunity for greater logical consistency between divine and human justice (otherwise it is difficult to exercise consistent justice when punishing someone for something that originated, either wholly or partially, with the Divine). The Christian view of the origin of evil is logically consistent. Because of the concept of evil as a privation, there is no conflict between the actual origin of evil and the benevolent, powerful characteristics of the God of mainstream Christianity. God remains good, and God remains powerful.

Furthermore, Christianity is consistent in asking adherents to resist evil and make improvements since evil does not originate from God. With regard to finding value in the human experience of evil, the Christian view is consistent as it allows room for one who suffers to hope for something better, which may aid one to persevere. One of the great strengths of the Christian position is that it does not embrace the hopelessness that is part of the opposing perspectives. These other views offer no good reason for one to hope for deterministic development of higher attributes such as patience, courage, and perseverance. In contrast to offering its adherents meaninglessness in suffering, Christianity provides the greatest amount of hope and value of any of the religions that are part of this study. This position allows people to develop coping mechanisms while going through evil experiences that in turn may help them endure evil experiences better (Fernandes, 2002a:128). It also allows people to develop higher-order virtues resulting from the experience of evil, such as courage, patience, and steadfastness. Going further, the Christian scriptures are clear that value not only *can* be had, but also *will* be had for the believer who experiences evil and suffering. James begins his letter by greeting those to whom he writes, and then immediately declares, "Consider it all joy, my brethren, when you encounter various trials" (James 1:2). Paul gives an indication of why one could consider it joy to face trials when he writes, "And we know that God causes all things to work together for good to those who love God, to those who are called according to His purpose" (Romans 8:28). The beatitudes given by Christ indicate blessings and rewards for those who are poor and those who hunger, mourn, and are persecuted (Matthew 5:3-11; Luke 6:20-22). This is a significant departure from the other theistic faiths because Christianity teaches that God *determines* to bring about goodness from circumstances of evil and suffering for everyone who follows Him, even though He did not determine to create the specific evil circumstances. God remains the source of goodness as He is the deterministic (purposeful) source of value in the experiences of evil. Further, one may argue that His determinism in making good come out of evil increases both His sovereignty and goodness, and this further increases its logical consistency. Christianity's view does not imply that its adherents ought to seek out experiences of evil or suffering; rather, it is an acknowledgment that these experiences, while undesirable, can lead to value for those who have suffered evil. This overall view is consistent when compared to the other aspects of Christianity's view of evil and suffering.

The defeat of evil is an intrinsic part of any religion's plan of salvation or its equivalent (such as enlightenment). The Christian paradigm is explicit in declaring that God must ultimately be the one to conquer evil. By contrast, the other faiths are equally explicit in their positions that offer varying degrees of opposition. It is no surprise that the other religions lean toward the view that humanity must conquer evil. In many ways, this view appears to be consistent with human development and humanity's sense of achievement. There does not seem to be much about life that people have not conquered. The world's tallest peak has been scaled repeatedly, humankind has explored deep into the sea, settlers have transformed much of the surface of the earth, and a few select people have even set foot upon the moon. It even appears humanity is not far from putting someone on Mars. When one looks at the history of human achievement, evil and suffering may appear as just one more challenge that humanity will eventually conquer. However, this view stands in dire contrast to the obvious circumstances of the world. The previous century saw two world wars that engulfed the planet for many long years. Over sixty-five million people (both civilian and military) died during those two conflicts alone (Ziemke, 2008; Keylor, 2008). The Holocaust, the Rwandan genocide, the Khmer Rouge's slaughter, or the suffering of innocents in the Syrian civil war are just a few more of the many examples of humankind's evil, despite the supposed evolution and development of the human species. The world's justice systems may lend superficial support to the view that humankind can conquer evil, but in experiential contrast, rape, murder, and physical harm to others are common crimes perpetrated the world over.

Natural evils also persist. The Christmas Tsunami of 2004 killed over two hundred thousand people (Rivers, 2009). Hurricane Katrina struck the Gulf Coast of the United States less than a year later, the most destructive and expensive natural disaster in the history of the country (FEMA, 2006). In 2010 a devastating earthquake struck Haiti leaving an estimated death toll of three hundred thousand (Reuters, 2010). While advances have been made that help avoid or mitigate some portion of the suffering that results from these natural evils, humankind cannot stop the tectonic plates from slipping, hurricanes from occurring, or tsunamis from sweeping up and onto the world's shores. Humankind can only soften the blow from these natural disasters, but people and their institutions cannot stop them. Christianity offers an alternative to the unsupported, optimistic view that humanity will conquer evil. The Christian paradigm is that God will ultimately conquer evil. Humanity does not help and plays no significant role in this victory; it is all in God's hands. The previous three paradigms are the foundation for this view. First, evil is real; therefore, there is hope it can be conquered. If it were not real, then it would be strange to attempt to conquer it. Second, evil does not come from God. Rather, all that God created is good. Since evil is a privation that was not part of God's creative acts, it is logically consistent to claim that He can and ultimately will conquer. In fact, it would be inconsistent if He did not conquer it at some point. Third, God already demonstrates His sovereignty over all things (including evil) by promising to bring value out of the human experience of evil. He can work goodness in spite of the purest acts of evil, and this is also consistent with the view that He is able to conquer evil. If the Christian claims of a corrupted, inherited nature are true, then clearly humanity has no chance to conquer sin on its own, and this is consistent as well. Humans also cannot conquer the natural evils of the world. Despite the best efforts of the greatest minds, humans simply do not have the ability to make the world into a place of safety and security where no suffering or evil occurs as the result of natural processes. If one wishes to have legitimate hope for this world without natural evil, then the Creator must be the one to accomplish it, and this is seen in Christian eschatology with the new earth (Rev. 21:1). It is also logically consistent to argue that the God of mainstream Christian theism, who is omnipotent, omniscient, and omnibenevolent, must defeat evil and end suffering *at some point in time*, even if the victory has not been fully consummated yet. It would be incorrectly limiting to claim that God should have conquered evil by this exact moment in time, as the omniscient God is in the process of implementing His plan to create the best possible world (Geisler and Corduan, 2003:334; Fernandes, 2002a:125). It is logically consistent to claim that God will conquer the evil that humans cannot in His perfect timing.

As has been demonstrated, logical consistency is one of the strengths of the components of Christian theodicy as defined by the UCC. Acknowledgment of the actuality of evil in human experience is consistent with correspondence theory. To claim that evil is less than real is inconsistent with human experience. Privation avoids the contradiction of an all-good God creating evil, and it is logically consistent that an all-good God would want to conquer evil. Furthermore, it is logically consistent to believe that the same all-powerful, benevolent God would take the responsibility for its defeat upon Himself. Claiming finite humans cannot conquer evil is consistent with this line of thought. The infinite, all-good, all-powerful, all-knowing God is the ideal and most logical being to conquer evil. It is consistent for Christian theology to claim that this sovereign, loving, powerful God purposefully creates benefits for His followers when they suffer, even though He did not cause the suffering. The four aspects of the Christian paradigm are logically sufficient and do not give cause to doubt its sufficiency.

CHAPTER 15:

The Historical Consistency of the Christian Paradigm for Evil

HISTORICAL CONSISTENCY IS AN additional topic that is part of the examination of consistency within systems of thought regarding evil. Historical consistency is not deductive proof that something is correct, but it is a corollary point of interest. For example, if one believes the earliest scriptural writings are correct, then there should be a consistent, reputable view throughout history that they are correct. Throughout the centuries, nothing should change with regard to fundamentals communicated in the scriptures. Regarding the specific topic of evil, one should look at what the earliest people thought about evil and examine how those ideas changed or remained the same over time. With specific regard to Christian theology, the theodicy taught by the apostles should not contradict the early views of evil expressed in the Old Testament, and modern, mainstream forms of Christianity should not contradict apostolic teachings.

However, there is a challenge in this area as the theodicies of the cultures of origin (the ancient cultures of the Middle East) are not explicit. This is not surprising given the dearth of ancient writings on this topic that are available to modern scholars. As a result of this lack, it is difficult to discover much about the ancient theodicies. However, the lack of a technical theological language does not necessitate a lack of theologically styled thought or precision since images, rituals, myths, and symbols can accurately express theological, historical, and social considerations in cultures that existed before fully developed, written language (Eliade, 1958:10, 33; Bonhoeffer, 1997:53; Feder and Park, 1993:7). While there are many gaps in the apparent theodicies of ancient cultures, particularly if compared to the well-developed and documented mainstream religions in this study, two key points of interest emerge when one examines the ancient representations of evil.

First, the cultures of origin did not treat evil as illusory. It is clear that they considered evil to be a real force of serious concern, and it had a real impact on their lives and on their religious behaviors. An ancient example comes from Sumeria where the early epics tell of an underworld. This is a realm of the dead, and evil spirits reside there, although one ought not to equate it with the Christian concept of hell. This concept also existed in other ancient cultures (Sandars, 1972:27-28; Eliade, 1978:65; Feder and Park, 1993:3). Next, other ancient texts also offer deluge stories that are similar to the story of Noah. As in the story of Noah, the evil and sins of the people precipitate the devastation, or sometimes the imbalance created by human existence requires corrective action (Hendel, 1987:13-26; Frymer-Kensky, 1977:147-155; Eliade, 1978:63). This is consistent with the reality of evil that is a constant theme throughout the Old and New Testaments. The belief in the reality of evil continues as part of modern, mainstream Christian theodicy today. All of the ancient cultures taught both explicitly and implicitly about the reality of evil.

Second, there is a common theme throughout history about the conquering of evil. In demonstrating this, one should start by recognizing the ubiquitous symbolism of chaotic waters as a representation of evil. The theme of chaotic waters is scattered throughout texts of the ancient world as well as in the Old and New Testaments (from the second verse of the first chapter to the first verse of the second-to-last chapter of the Bible). Expanding the scope further, this symbolism is in the myths, rituals, and symbols of all the ancient cultures at the heart of their civilizations, and it has its roots in ancient modes of religious thought and expression. The creation stories of the ancient world speak of the divine conquering of a watery chaos, which is linked to the waters described in Genesis 1:2 (Deroche, 1992:11-12; Blythin, 1962:120-121; Lovell, 1955:271-274) and to the sea described in Daniel 7:2 (Gardner, 1999:412-414). Eliade observes the common theme of water as a destructive, chaotic, bad force in ancient modes of thought (1958:191-194; 1997:54), and Feder and Park draw attention to the shared Jewish and Christian story of creation as the story of a God who brings order to a watery chaos (1993:7). This mode of thought was also common in Egyptian stories, which sometimes used a symbol of the watery chaos, while other times the stories employed a more explicit reference to creating order over chaos. The Canaanite story of creation with Baal made use of the water-chaos imagery, as did the Hittites (Eliade, 1978:88-92, 156; 1957:77). In this common representation of evil, it is always the Divine (God or the supreme deity of the pantheon) who conquers the chaos-evil. Ra established *ma'at* (order) in the place of chaos (Eliade, 1978:91). This is seen in the establishment of solid land (the primordial mound) among the chaotic seas and is commemorated by the benben stone topping the famous pyramids. Baal killed Yam/ Prince Sea (Eliade, 1978:153-154), which is the personification of water-chaos-evil. In Christianity it is God who conquers chaos-evil; humanity never conquers it. In ancient cultures, the creative act of the Divine (conquering the chaos-evil, establishing order/existence) is the first act of goodness (with regard to humans) as this is what makes human life possible (Odell-Hein, 2007:72-73). This view can also be discerned in the theologies of both Augustine and Aquinas, both of whom deal with the concepts of the goodness of God as revealed in the creation story as well as God's establishment of order (as opposed to primordial chaos/nonexistence) or the degree of goodness in existence (Augustine, 1961:148; Aquinas, 1989:19).

This early theme of evil-chaos is scattered throughout the Old Testament, starting with the waters described in the creation story (Genesis 1:2). The theme is also in the passages that refer to the sea beast that God battles (Psalm 74:13-14, Job 26:12-13, and Isaiah 51:9 are just a few examples) since the beast is a personification of the chaotic waters. While the concept of water-chaos-evil is not unique to Christianity, the New Testament is unique in that it makes use of the theme with both an incarnate deity as well as in an eschatological solution. When the waters rage, it is Christ who commands the waters to calm, and they do (Matthew 8:23-26). When the disciples are sitting in a boat in the middle of the sea, Christ calmly walks on the water's stormy surface (Matthew 14:25; Mark 6:48; John 6:19). Consistent with ancient thought, this is something only the supreme Deity can do, and both of these stories symbolically present Christ as the one who conquers the water-chaos-evil. As Christ is God, this is consistent with the ancient view that only God can conquer the water-chaos-evil. In the book of Revelation, the image of water-chaos-evil emerges again when the enemy of God rises up out of the sea: "Then I saw a beast coming up out of the sea, having ten horns and seven heads, and on his horns were ten diadems, and on his heads were blasphemous names" (Revelation 13:1b). Later, near the end of the book, the final instance of this imagery occurs at the point when the new heaven and the new earth—both perfected and *free from evil*—are revealed to John. This passage would seem curiously out of place if not for the context provided by the ancient mode of thought regarding evil and chaos. "Then I saw a new heaven and a new earth, for the first heaven and the first earth had passed away, *and there was no longer any sea*" (Revelation 21:1; emphasis added). A full treatment of this topic falls outside the scope of this study, but it is clear that from the first appearance of the water-chaos-evil in the story of creation to its final elimination in the eschaton, God's promise remains: He will conquer the evil that afflicts humanity.

The historical consistency of the other two main topics (the origin of evil and value in the human experience of evil) is debatable. It is difficult to discern a firm position among the beliefs of the ancient cultures because of the absence of detailed records on the topic. With regard to the origin of evil, there is precious little agreement on the topic. In many cases, this appears to be a non-issue since the aforementioned waters of chaos pre-exist creation with no agreed-upon explanation of their origin. There are many variations on this topic; therefore, one cannot accurately claim any historical consistency. With regard to the value in the human experience of evil, there is even less material on this topic in the ancient writings than there is on the origin of evil.

Only two of the four components of the paradigm for Christian theodicy have enough of an established, ancient root to be able to check for historical consistency. However, Christianity is historically consistent with regard to the two components that one is able to discern from ancient times: evil as reality and the divine conquering of evil. Furthermore, the general patterns of Christian thought have remained consistent from the time of the Patriarchs, to the co-authors of the Bible in both the Old and New Testaments, and into modern, mainstream Christian theology. Christian theodicy has not evolved inconsistently over time. Rather, it displays overall consistency through history.

CHAPTER 16:

The Theological Consistency of the Christian Paradigm for Evil

IN ORDER FOR A specific view to be sufficient, it must not contradict the other various theological components of the overall faith, otherwise an adherent or potential believer has reason to doubt or reject it. If Christian theodicy is not consistent with the other portions of mainstream Christian theology (such as soteriology, eschatology, hamartiology, Christology, etc.), then one may question or even reject the sufficiency of its theodicy.

The first point to consider is the reality of evil. In mainstream Christian theodicy, both evil and people are real. The suffering they experience is real. This is consistent with both human experience and with the other areas of Christian theology. This is in contradistinction to some positions that claim individual selves are not real or that evil is not real. Correspondence theory indicates otherwise. All aspects of mainstream Christian theology (including soteriology, anthropology, theology proper, Christology, pneumatology, eschatology, and others) teach that people and circumstances are part of reality (Grudem, 1994; Erickson, 1998).

It is also theologically consistent to claim that evil does not come from God. Once Adam sinned, evil took hold in the world. This matches the Christian claim that God wishes to reconcile people to Him. Rather than sending evil to lead people astray, God attempts to bring healing and deliverance to people (Boyd, 2003:14-15; Phillips, 1991:111) and to draw them into a saving relationship with Him. If evil came from God, it would be inconsistent with His desire for people to be in a pure, holy relationship with Him. But, since evil comes from humans, there is no theological contradiction, and it is consistent. This also aligns consistently with the doctrine that there is value in the human experience of evil. God is omnipotent, omniscient, and omnibenevolent. Only a God with those characteristics, who also did not create evil (Fernandes, 2000:48) but wants to redeem people from it (Henry, 1999:303; Boyd, 2003:61; Rice, 1994:44-46), is consistent in promising value from the trials and suffering people experience from evil. The position of Christian theodicy that posits God as the conqueror of evil further strengthens its overall theological consistency. He does not force people to conquer it themselves, and they cannot even if they desire to do so. Soteriology addresses the issue of how people are unable to conquer sin in achieving salvation and victory over evil. "By the works of the Law no flesh will be justified in His sight" (Romans 3:20). God redeems people; they do not redeem themselves. This is consistent with a loving God who truly desires reconciliation with His people. This also points to God's proactive approach to reconciling people to Him and to conquering evil. Contrast this with Hinduism, where the ultimate deity emanates maya and takes no action to aid people in conquering it, or contrast it with Judaism, where God will redeem the world, but only after people have made it worthy of His redemptive acts (Heschel, 1976:348, 379-380). In both cases God is either partly or largely responsible for evil, but people must conquer it themselves, which appears contradictory (people conquering the will of the Divine). In Christian soteriology and hamartiology,

God intervenes in the world to conquer the evil that He did not will or create, and He makes redemption possible, even though not a single individual can make himself worthy. Passages from both the Old and New Testaments make this clear. "There is no one who does good, not even one" (Psalms 14:3, 53:1), and "all have sinned and fall short of the glory of God" (Romans 3:23).

Mainstream Christian theodicy is theologically consistent. Thus, there is no reason for one to doubt the sufficiency of the Christian paradigm. In addition to logical and historical consistency, the paradigm offered by Christian theodicy is workable and sufficient. The various parts of Christian theology work together to provide an explanation and solution for evil that one can acknowledge as a possible, adequate solution. One may have reason to doubt that humans will ever conquer evil (the current state of the world is enough to cause doubt). However, one cannot deny the workability of the Christian paradigm: an all-loving, all-powerful, all-knowing God will conquer a real evil that did not originate with Him.

CHAPTER 17:

The Experiential Consistency of the Christian Paradigm for Evil

AS LAID OUT IN the first chapter of this study, the experiential component of evil and suffering is an important component to consider regarding theodicy. Religions must be able to address this issue adequately for its adherents, and they all address it in their own unique ways. These are significant points of differentiation since they speak directly to the (improperly perceived or actual) experiences of evil that an adherent suffers. For the Christian, the existence of self is existentially undeniable (Geisler and Brooks, 1990:139). God created humans; they have real, physical senses; and Christ came, died, and rose in physical, human form (Grudem, 1994:532-535, 609-613; Wright, 2003:668; Philippians 2:5-8; Luke 24:36-43). Existential undeniability naturally leads to the application of the correspondence theory of truth. In this view, it is not only consistent but also necessary for one to posit that one's experiences are also existentially real and important, and that these experiences have a degree of truthfulness intrinsic in their actuality. For theodicy, this means that if one experiences evil, then it is a real experience, and it is a true, meaningful, and impactful experience. One ought not to marginalize or ignore it. This lends further support to the view that God can make some value come out of experiences of evil. Since these are real experiences, potentiality exists for actual change and benefit. This also falls in line with human perception. People perceive pain and suffering, which implicitly tells them that it is valid to acknowledge those experiences as true and meaningful. This validates human actions taken to minimize or prevent those experiences. It is consistent with mainstream Christian theism's existential undeniability and it is compliant with correspondence theory. Much of what could be covered in this section was covered earlier, and so it will not be re-covered in more detail here. When all of the information is considered, the paradigm offered by Christian theodicy is experientially consistent.

Summary of the Consistency of the Christian Paradigm for Evil

In order for a particular theodicy to be sufficient for its followers, it needs to be consistent because a lack of consistency provides a reason to doubt or reject a particular view. This study examined the logical, historical, theological, and experiential consistencies of the Christian position, and it demonstrated that mainstream Christian theodicy is fully consistent in each area. This consistency enables one to acknowledge the Christian approach as a workable, sufficient possibility. Note that sufficiency is not proof of truth, and it is not a demonstration of superiority. However, it allows one to consider the possibility that the Christian view is true and workable. The next step is to move beyond sufficiency in order to look at what differentiates Christian theodicy from other theodicies that also claim sufficiency.

Introduction to Uniqueness of Christian Theodicy

At this point, the focus shifts away from looking at the sufficiency of the Christian position and focuses on the unique aspects of Christian theodicy. Christian theodicy is clearly unique in terms of being the only religion in this study that makes use of the *anthroactual/purposeful-hieroredemptive* system identified by the UCC, but it must be unique in more than just the basic, comparative differences between the various paradigms. While these differences are important, simply being different does not necessarily elevate a particular theodicy to a higher level. It is also not enough for a theodicy to be merely sufficient; in order to make a persuasive argument for one to become an adherent, something must draw people toward embracing one particular theodicy over all other sufficient options. Mainstream Christian theodicy's unique aspects elevate it beyond mere sufficiency toward a view that is compelling, desirable, and inimitable. When one looks to the compelling, unique aspects of Christian theodicy, one must look at four specific areas: historicity and valorization, assurance, exclusivity, and participation.

CHAPTER 18:

Historicity And Valorization

A LARGE DIFFERENCE BETWEEN the various religions and their theodicies is whether they embrace linear or cyclical views of time and existence. One of the key factors in Eastern religions such as Hinduism and Buddhism is the use of cyclical time (Eliade, 1954:112-118). In these views, time goes through successive cycles as ages repeat over and again (Michaels, 2004:300; Prakash, 1955:499). This is particularly impactful with respect to the experiences of an individual adherent. For that individual, once a cycle of time completes, a new cycle of time replaces it. Once that cycle completes, another one will occur, and so on. In the end, there are many cycles of time that follow each other in succession, and each one resets and overwrites (to varying degrees) what has happened previously. In practical terms for adherents of these faiths, if one does not achieve enlightenment (overcome evil) in one's current lifetime, then there are many future opportunities (in the form of personal reincarnations) to achieve enlightenment (Gethin, 1998:7, 27-28; Das, 1998:110-115). Also, if one faces a circumstance and chooses the path of evil, then in a successive cycle of time one may face the same or a similar circumstance again. If the adherent makes a different choice this time, it effectively replaces the previous choice. While the karma affects subsequent cycles (Gethin, 1998:119; Good 2000:281; Morgan 2001:34-35; Creel 1972:161; Shulman, 1979:652), ultimately it does not matter whether one takes just a few or several thousand incarnations to achieve enlightenment. Once one achieves enlightenment, the previous cycles are irrelevant (as if they never existed), and the actions and experiences of each incarnation matter for nothing in the end. Eliade refers to this view of time in religion as "cyclical time" or the "regeneration of time" (2005:51-92).

This is a point where the particulars of Christian theodicy differ significantly. In direct opposition to the cyclical views of time, mainstream expressions of theism, dating back to early Judaism, make use of linear time that is both irreversible and historical (Eliade, 1954:104-105). In this view, time is not cyclical, and one's life does not repeat. That which happens in linear time is granted an increased level of significance by nature of it happening only once and never being replaced—there is no benefit of cyclical time that would allow one to redo, undo, mitigate, or redeem the actions of a previous cycle as if they had not occurred. It is, as Eliade phrases it, "one-way time" (1954:104). This has an important effect on the philosophy of religion as it naturally increases the significance of all human deeds and historical events because of their singularity and permanence (historicity). It also increases the significance of actions performed by God in historical time as history itself is largely a series of historical theophanies (Eliade, 1954:104-107). The activities and their results in this historical, actual, linear time line of existence are important enough to God for Him to participate and intervene in them. With regard to evil and suffering, He even takes steps to conquer them through observable, historical action. As opposed to religions that take advantage of cyclical time, in which a successive cycle of time can render all previous actions meaningless, Christian theodicy engages in historical, linear time where actions and experiences are of utmost and eternal meaning. Therefore, one's sins are significant in that they are permanent—no successive cycle of time will allow someone a "do over." Linear history permanently records all acts of evil as such, and there is no subsequent reboot of time that replaces these acts of evil. In Christianity, the Bible speaks of human sins in both the past and future tense as facts (Romans 3:22-23; Schaeffer, 1998:77-78). These are facts that humans will not replace or overwrite by subsequent actions. As previously demonstrated, this same historicity of the events that one faces and the choices one makes lends itself toward development of eternal attributes as there is no subsequent existence that renders suffering, perseverance, or development irrelevant. Historicity demands all human actions and experiences to be of eternal value. This historicity also makes the acts of God in time very significant. Christian theodicy is unique and compelling partly because God made a choice to take historical, temporal action to defeat evil and suffering with the incarnation, sacrifice, and resurrection of Christ (Erickson 1998:475; Flora 1992:15; Clendenin, 1988: 325-326). The acts of God maintain significance relative to their historicity and to the historicity of human choices and experiences.

Building on the foundation of historicity, the physical, human incarnation of God in time is of unique and compelling significance. Other theistic faiths have a picture of a god who intervenes, to some extent, in human affairs, but is never incarnate in human form. Hinduism offers a wide range of divine incarnations, but since every incarnation is a form of limited multiplicity, no incarnation of a god is a full revelation of truth; it is just a single, limited, flawed perspective. But in mainstream Christian theology, God's incarnation (Philippians 2:5-8) is significant because it communicates the value God places on physically existent humanity. God does not offer a plan of salvation and escape from evil that causes one to discard the physical, temporal body as does Buddhism, Hinduism, and other related faiths. Rather, God participated in the physicality that He created.

God's valuation of the physical existence that He created is consistent throughout scripture. God created a physical world that he judged as "good" (Genesis 1:4-25) and He created physical, historical beings to live in it (Adam and Eve). He judged His entire creation as "very good" (Genesis 1:31). After creation, God intervened in the physical, temporal lives of people throughout history. When it came time for the greatest of interventions, Jesus became incarnate—fully God and *fully human.* The two natures of divinity and humanity are not partial or blended. This is the point of the Christian doctrine known as *hypostatic union* (Moreland and Craig, 2003:600-602; Grudem, 1994:556-560). Fully human includes the concept of physicality. When Jesus died on a cross at Calvary, it was a real, physical, bodily death (Erickson, 1998:790-791). His subsequent resurrection was a physical, bodily resurrection (Grudem, 1994:608-613). Everything about Christ's incarnation expressed in the gospels takes place in historical, temporal, bodily form. God's decisive actions take place on the same existential plane as humanity. This is also true of Christianity's eschatology. Christ's return is a bodily return as an objective, historical event that takes place in objective history among physical people (Revelation 19:11-22:5). The afterlife for humanity is not a ghostly, disembodied existence, but rather it is a physical existence on the physical new earth. In addition, people receive their glorified bodies, which are physical, temporal bodies that are free from the effects of evil and sin. Everything about God's plan for humanity falls within the context of some form of history, physical existence, or reality (Alcorn, 2004:111-118, 241-310; Grudem, 1994:1159-1162). This is unique and compelling because this elevates the value of humanity when compared with other religions. No other faith offers a God who is as concerned with physical humanity. He became incarnate as a member of humanity. As part of this, He experienced the trials of life as all humans do. The author of Hebrews emphasized it when he wrote about Christ, "For we do not have a high priest who cannot sympathize with our weaknesses, but One who has been tempted in all things as we are" (Hebrews 4:15).

The Christian doctrine of the God who became incarnate valorizes human existence. The physical, temporal existence is not necessarily evil or undesirable, as Jesus was fully human (physical and temporal) and entirely without sin. Too many adherents miss this point and tend toward a Christo-Platonic or ancient Gnostic view, which holds that the physical form is somehow less valued and less desirable (Alcorn, 2004:112-113; Turner, 1990:199-200). Because God has placed high value on humanity's physical, temporal existence, and because He became incarnate and performed actions and deeds in the physically existent world, the actions and deeds of each individual have value as well.

The impact of the Christian view, properly applied, is significant. Each life has significant value. All actions an individual performs have significant value. The historicity of actions and experiences allows for increased meaning and eternal benefit. Furthermore, God can empathize with human struggles, trials, suffering, and the experience of evil, something that no other god can truly claim. God promises to rectify that which has gone wrong (evil and sin) without destroying the physical existence He intended for people; rather, He perfects it.

CHAPTER 19:

Assurance

MOST RELIGIONS OFFER AN approach to evil that promises some form of future deliverance to their adherents. However, there is little evidence available to people that substantiates, guarantees, or offers concrete hope that the promised deliverance will come to pass. For example, Judaism promises a future time of redemption, at which point God will conquer the remaining evils, both spiritual and impulse-based evils. However, Judaism offers this future event based on the presumption that positive human action will occur in sufficient quality and quantity as to merit God's final intervention and redemption (Heschel, 1976:348, 379-380). This theology states two things. First, it teaches that humans are capable of earning redemption. Second, it teaches that at some point in the future, God will redeem the world because humans have fulfilled their potential to earn redemption. However, there is a large, unfilled gap between the first and second points. Judaism's theology offers no concrete evidence that bridges the chasm between human potential for widespread righteousness and the actualization of that potential. In fact, given the state of the world, with crimes against humanity, wars, poverty, and suffering, one might argue that the only evidence that exists actually supports an opposing view. The same is true of the other religions. Islam offers no more concrete reason for hope of redemption than Judaism. It also promises a future time of redemption and in the meantime offers Islamicization as a way to fight many of the evils in the world. Mainstream Buddhism offers two distinct views, both of which offer a promise of enlightenment on some level. Theravada Buddhism generally states that it is up to an individual to achieve enlightenment (Das, 1998:62-63). However, there is no guarantee that any individual will ever achieve enlightenment, let alone on a widespread scale. By contrast, Mahayana traditions claim that all people can achieve enlightenment, and that at some point enlightenment will indeed occur for all people (Das, 1998:143, 370). However, as with Judaism, the gap between potentiality and actuality is wide and unexplained; one must simply assume that it will happen with no evidence to back up the assumption. Hinduism describes a natural cycle that lasts billions of years, and at the end of the cycle all is one with the Brahman, at least until the next time (Michaels, 2004:300; Prakash, 1955:499). However, one must take this strictly on faith, and only then with the understanding that even this cycle must again repeat itself (which necessitates the re-emergence of evil). These faiths offer a vague future that is free from evil; yet, there is no logical reason for an adherent to believe that the wonderful future described by each religion will move from vague promise to concrete actuality.

Christian theodicy offers something substantial to its adherents in this area. As with these other religions, Christian theodicy promises a future elimination of evil, but it claims that this elimination of evil is more than just a vague promise; the historical life and actions of Jesus guarantee the promised future. One early biblical example of the reality of God's promises coming to pass was when God spoke to Abraham, and told him to "'look toward the heavens, and count the stars, if you are able to count them.' And He said to him, 'So shall your descendants be'" (Genesis 15:5). Later, He again promised that "I will multiply you exceedingly" (Genesis 17:3) and "I have made you the father of a multitude of nations" (Genesis 17:5). As more than just vague promises of a future condition, God gave His promises historical, objective significance through the birth of Isaac at a time of life when both Abraham and Sarah were at a significantly advanced age and did not expect to conceive and bear children. In this vibrant example, God gave Abraham a concrete reason to believe that He would fulfill His promise. In a different example, God made a promise to David about his line of descendants and the rule of Israel. "Your house and your kingdom shall endure before Me forever; your throne shall be established forever" (2 Samuel 7:16). God actualized His promise, as the Messiah traces His heritage through both Mary and Joseph back to David (Schaeffer, 1998:16-17). The messianic promises continue as Gabriel delivers a message from God to Daniel where He specifies the period of time that must pass until the time of the Messiah, who is the descendant of David that will rule forever. "From the issuing of a decree to restore and rebuild Jerusalem until Messiah the Prince there will be seven weeks and sixty-two weeks" (Daniel 9:25). This is a twofold prophecy. First, there is a prophecy of a future decree to restore and rebuild Jerusalem. If that portion of the prophecy goes unfulfilled, then there is no reason to believe the remainder of the prophecy. God fulfilled the first portion in concrete, objective fashion with Artaxerxes I's decree of 444, dated to 1 Nisan on the Jewish calendar or 5 March on the Gregorian calendar (Nehemiah 2:5-8). This partial fulfillment gave people concrete reason to believe that the remaining portion of the prophecy would come true. God then fulfilled the remaining half of the promise with the triumphal entry of Jesus into Jerusalem, which is an exact match for the length of time that needed to elapse between Artaxerxes I's decree and Jesus' entry into the city (McDowell, 1979:170-174). Once again, God made a promise, and He fulfilled it in objective history. While God requires faith, He has shown that He will fulfill His promises to people in an actual, meaningful, experiential manner. God does not require blind faith at the expense of logic; rather, His appeal for faith comes at least partially through rationality and reason (Schaeffer, 1998:37-42). The combination of promise and historicity is potent as it gives adherents concrete, rational, logical reasons to believe, hope, and persevere.

Likewise, God's eschatological promise of a final defeat of evil offers a believer assurance of its fulfillment based on the historicity and actuality of His former actions. God fulfilled His promises to His people in an objective, historical fashion. The Messiah came to be among His people as more than just a spiritual presence; He came to conquer evil and redeem humanity in historical time and in human form. God's official conquering of evil (the victory during the most critical battle) does not take place in some nebulous future that adherents may only speculate about or hope to exist. Jesus' sacrificial death and subsequent historical, bodily resurrection is the key component in the defeat of evil. Evil lost the critical battle in objective, historical fashion at Christ's cross and empty tomb; the forces of darkness cannot ultimately prevail (Clendenin, 1988:325-326; Wright, 2006:94, 136-137; Weatherhead, 1972:15; Erickson, 1998:475; Flora, 1992:15). The Christian believer does not have to rely on a vague, unsupported hope of victory based on a promise with no assurance. Instead, the Christian adherent is able to look to God's historical, bodily action for assurance that He has already won the key victory over evil (even if God has not yet fully implemented His victory by eliminating it entirely from the present world).

Furthermore, Christ resurrected *bodily* (Grudem, 1994:608-613) and appeared physically before many witnesses. Paul wrote of this in his first letter to the church at Corinth.

> For I delivered to you as of first importance what I also received, that Christ died for our sins according to the Scriptures, He was buried, and that He was raised on the third day according to the Scriptures,

> and that He appeared to Cephas, then to the twelve. After that He appeared to more than five hundred brethren at one time, most of whom remain until now, but some have fallen asleep; then He appeared to James, then to all the apostles; and last of all, as to one untimely born, He appeared to me also (1 Corinthians 15:3-8).

The bodily resurrection and widespread public, objective, and historical encounters with the resurrected Christ are assurances of God's acceptance of Christ's sacrifice as sufficient. Without this, then any promise of a physical, bodily future that is free from evil (sin and death) is suspect and leaves one without assurance.

> But if there is no resurrection of the dead, not even Christ has been raised; and if Christ has not been raised, then our preaching is vain, your faith also is vain. Moreover we are even found to be false witnesses of God, because we testified against God that He raised Christ, whom He did not raise, if in fact the dead are not raised. For if the dead are not raised, not even Christ has been raised; and if Christ has not been raised, your faith is worthless; you are still in your sins. Then those also who have fallen asleep in Christ have perished (1 Corinthians 15:13-18).

As further evidence of this concept, the Bible records a related event that took place in the physical, historical time of Jesus' death and resurrection. "The tombs were opened, and many bodies of the saints who had fallen asleep were raised, and coming out of the tombs after His resurrection they entered the holy city and appeared to many" (Matthew 27:52-53). This historical event provides further evidence of God's claims and gives the believer assurance for the defeat of evil and the redemption of the faithful. God's resurrection of the dead proved that Jesus' sacrifice was sufficient and that death was conquered. The debate between Pharisees and Sadducees about the resurrection of the dead was answered with an objective, physical event. Believers can look to objective history to see concrete proof of God's power to raise the dead and provide an afterlife.

The mainstream Christian adherent has more than vague hope for a nebulous eschatological state. Rather, God has acted to fulfill His promises in historical time, and these actions provide concrete evidence that He actualizes His will in temporal, human existence. The sacrifice and resurrection of Jesus in historical time is proof that evil is conquered and humankind may experience redemption and reconciliation.

CHAPTER 20:

Exclusivity

SOME RELIGIONS CLAIM TO be inclusive, some claim to be exclusive, and others fall somewhere in between. Christianity lays claim to strong exclusivity, which provides a clear path for an adherent to follow. By contrast, the other theistic faiths claim some degree of openness with regard to who is included in their final solution for conquering evil, as it is largely based on one's good deeds outweighing one's bad deeds (Surah 39.70, 40.17, 41.46; Nasr, 2003:72-73; Ali, 1990:38, 210; Smith H., 1991:242; Ariel, 1995:19, 101; Heschel, 1976:382-383; Brener, 2004:193). Some hold up Buddhism as attempting to be compatible with other religions instead of excluding good people of other faiths, for example, a Catholic that can also be a Buddhist (Das, 1998:14-17). These mixed messages can be confusing for a prospective adherent. These religions teach that there is a specific path to salvation or enlightenment based on specific scriptures, traditions, and behaviors. However, an individual has leeway so long as one does not deviate into heresy (such as a Muslim embracing the doctrine of the Trinity). These approaches do not offer a single, clear soteriological path leading toward the desired eschatological state. Further, the allowable amount and type of deviance from the base path is not explicit, apart from the issue of obvious heresy. Therefore, clarity for both theology and practical living is lost.

Hinduism takes a different approach to inclusivity. It is rooted in the monistic philosophy that lies at the core of the religion. This view claims that since all is one, all perceived deities are really just the singular God-Brahman. The path of bhakti devotionalism claims that true, devoted worship of any perceived god is ultimately worship of the truly existent, singular God-Brahman (Morgan, 2001:71; Smith H., 1991:36). As a result of this monistic view, truly devoted worship of any god (a devotee must choose one, specific god to be devoted to) can lead to enlightenment since it all resolves to worship the God-Brahman (Nath, 2001:42; Morgan, 2001:72; Narayanan, 2003:145; Renard, 2002:262). However, this claim is false and deceptive. It demonstrates a significant misunderstanding (or complete disregard for) the foundational world-view of theistic faiths. Much of the scriptural support for this Hindu view is in the Bhagavad Gita. The chief speaker in the Bhagavad Gita is the Hindu god Krishna, and he is teaching the mortal Arjuna about the true nature of the world. Arjuna is having a crisis of conscience just as he is about to enter battle. He does not want to kill worthy adversaries and end good lives, which would create pain and sorrow for their surviving families (Bhagavad Gita 1.17-47). Krishna responds by informing Arjuna that he should be indifferent to the results of his actions (and whom he maims or kills) in battle (Bhagavad Gita 2.1-50). Krishna proceeds to explain to Arjuna the true nature of reality, existence, and the gods. What follows is a series of lectures explaining how all the seemingly different gods are manifestations of the one, true God (Brahman), and that all it takes is *self*less devotion to any one of them in order to achieve liberation and enlightenment. However, a previous part of this study demonstrated that acceptance of duality (God transcends and is separate from creation) or multiplicity (the belief in several distinct, actual existences as opposed to the monistic view) prevents liberation in Hinduism. However, duality and multiplicity are required in theistic faiths due to the nature of the truly existent Divine that is separate from creation as well as from several distinct, real people (van Baaren, 2008; Wainwright, 2005). The bhakti-devotionalist view may attempt to work around this theistic obstacle by saying that devotion to any god leads to liberation, including the deities worshipped in all other faiths (including theistic religions). Unfortunately, that simply does not acknowledge the requisite views of theism that require duality and multiplicity. The contradiction in the Hindu path of devotion with regard to theism remains unresolved because Hinduism does not adequately address it. However, one may gain clarity with regard to this problem in a careful reading of the Bhagavad Gita. At the start of chapter nine, Krishna informs Arjuna that he will reveal the secret of life as well as how to be free from suffering. In doing this, Krishna declares a precondition for liberation: "*those who are without faith in my teaching, cannot attain me*; they endlessly return to this world, shuttling from death to death" (9.1-3; emphasis added). Attaining Krishna is liberation (enlightenment, victory over evil), and those who cannot attain him are clearly subject to reincarnation and the continued illusion of self (perpetuated evil). In case there is any doubt about what constitutes "my teaching," which is a prerequisite for liberation, in the next verse Krishna begins a long, detailed explanation of Hinduism's monistic philosophy, beginning with "I permeate the entire universe in my unmanifest form. All beings exist within me" (9.4). He then teaches the unmistakable Hindu doctrine of Brahman and singularity (9.4-19). When the whole of Krishna's teachings in the Bhagavad Gita are considered, devotion to any one, specific god is indeed a valid path to liberation *but only if the devotee fully accepts a monistic doctrine*. By Krishna's own words, if this monistic philosophy is not accepted, then the devotee who embraces dualism will still be subject to samsara and not achieve liberation (9.3). Mainstream theistic faiths do not accept monism; therefore, any true theist will fall into Krishna's category of "those who are without faith in my teaching," and they will not achieve liberation. Likewise, fringe "theists" whose beliefs and practices fall outside of mainstream theism, such as those who choose instead to embrace syncretistic, mystical expressions of quasi-theism and universalist soteriological views, are not practicing full devotion to their deity as prescribed by Krishna (full, unwavering devotion to YWHW, the Triune God, or Allah). Therefore, they travel a path that is something other than the path of true, focused devotion required for liberation. A careful reading of the Hindu scriptures reveals that one must accept the core doctrine required by all Hindu paths: the ultimate goal of union with the God-Brahman. Only if one holds to a monistic view does devotion to any monistically based deity result in victory over evil. Although Hinduism tries deceptively to present this view as inclusive or universal, it is far from it.

By contrast, mainstream Christian theodicy is openly exclusive, and its doctrines and scriptures are clear in their exclusivity. Evil exists; it is real, and only the Triune God of the Christian Bible can conquer it (Jesus' sacrifice and resurrection has already won the decisive victory). No amount of good deeds can conquer evil and save a person. "A man is not justified by the works of the Law but through faith in Christ Jesus . . . since *by the works of the Law shall no man be justified*" (Galatians 2:16, emphasis added). Worship of any other god will not suffice, and worship of a false, monistic view of Christ (though invoking His name) is invalid faith. "Those who worship Him must worship in spirit and *truth*" (John 4:24, emphasis added). The concept of truth in this passage indicates that one must worship the true God and not some clearly false view of God that just makes use of Christian nomenclature. Jesus himself declares,

> Not everyone who says to Me, 'Lord, Lord,' will enter the kingdom of heaven . . . Many will say to Me on that day, 'Lord, Lord, did we not prophesy in Your name, and in Your name cast out demons, and

> in Your name perform many miracles?' And then I will declare to them, I never knew you; depart from me, you who practice lawlessness (Matthew 7:21-23).

Those whose beliefs violate explicit biblical teachings about the nature of God or those whose religious behaviors are in clear violation of scripture are those "who practice lawlessness" and will not be saved regardless of their use of the name of the Christ. Jesus was explicit with His exclusive claim: "I am the way, and the truth, and the life; *no one* comes to the Father but *through Me*" (John 14:6, emphasis added).

Christian theodicy makes clear claims of truth in support of its exclusive soteriology. The Christian scriptures declare that Jesus is the only way to salvation. Only those who believe in and follow Him will participate in the eschatological victory over evil. Nothing changes that and no one receives an exception. By grace through faith in Jesus alone will one be able to partake in God's victory over evil. The Bible is clear in its exclusivity. Mainstream expressions of Christianity do not deviate from this view. This clarity and precision is a unique and compelling advantage for one who truly seeks a clear path for the defeat of evil. This is yet another form of theological consistency, and while it is exclusive, the necessary path that an adherent must pursue is clear, easy to understand, and open to all who will accept it. It is a universal invitation to an exclusive faith.

CHAPTER 21:

Participation

THE FINAL UNIQUE AREA discussed in this study is participation. All religions have varying degrees of human participation in the divine plan. Buddhism and Hinduism do not just invite human participation in the defeat of evil, they demand that humanity defeats it. Islam and Judaism also require deeds of people in conquering evil. Christianity, as mentioned earlier, does not require the deeds of humanity to overcome evil, and human works do not affect God's ultimate conquering of evil. This doctrine is unique and should be compelling for potential adherents. However, while God does not need human involvement, He offers believing humans an opportunity for short-term blessings and long-term rewards by participating in His will. God's will does not need human action. He can provide for the hungry, heal the sick, and cause revelation leading to salvation without the aid of any particular person. However, He offers people a participatory (not necessary) role in the execution of His will. God can provide food without the aid of other people, as in the example of Elijah in the desert (1 Kings 17:1-6). He can extend life without doctors or people with healing ministries, such as with Hezekiah (2 Kings 20:1-11). He can minister to those in prison, or those who are being tortured or killed, without the involvement of people, such as what happened with the fiery furnace or with the apostles in prison (Daniel 3:1-19; Acts 12:1-11). However, His followers are instructed to feed the hungry, tend to the sick, visit those in prison (Matthew 25:34-40) and also to take care of widows and orphans (James 1:27). While God does not need human participation to make these things happen, Jesus equated these actions to serving and taking care of Himself, which is high praise. "To the extent that you did it to one of these brothers of Mine, even the least of them, you did it to Me" (Matthew 25:40). He promises great, eternal rewards for those who participate in this manner (Matthew 25:34). With regard to spreading the Gospel, Jesus commands adherents to "make disciples of all the nations" (Matthew 28:19). An individual adherent's action (or inaction) does not limit God in this regard, but He does invite that adherent to participate in the blessing of carrying the good news of salvation to others. Though discipleship is not a deed that earns salvation, it is one of the most important callings given to a Christian, one that Paul writes of in his letter to the Romans (Romans 10:14-15). To spread the truth of God's plan of salvation and deliverance from evil is a privilege for Christian adherents. Also, while God does not require human assistance in conquering evil during the eschaton, He does reward those who participate faithfully in His will, such as the martyrs who reign with Christ for a thousand years (Revelation 20:4). God is ultimately in control of providing for the needy, healing the sick, bringing redemption to the lost, and defeating the evil that plagues the world. This is where the generosity and love of God shines through in unique and compelling fashion. Unlike the other religions, Christian theodicy does not place on humans the burden of conquering these three areas and relieving suffering and evil. However, it does not entirely absolve humans from participation, and it offers great rewards to those who do participate. This is a unique balance. The opportunity to participate in something controlled by God and guaranteed to succeed, with full blessings and rewards, demonstrates a vast difference from the theology and theodicy of other religions, and it is another unique and appealing aspect of Christian theodicy.

Summary of the Uniqueness of Christian Theodicy

The mainstream Christian system for dealing with evil and suffering is sufficient and consistent. These last few chapters demonstrated the variety of ways in which Christian theodicy moves beyond sufficiency toward something that is unique and compelling. Historicity and valorization is the view of action in linear time that provides a foundation for true and meaningful experiences. God's promises and their fulfillment in real time provide a substantial reason for hope, and Christ's sacrifice and resurrection defeated evil and guarantees the eventual culmination of its elimination. God's participation in humanity via temporal intervention and human incarnation valorizes human existence and actions to a level far beyond that of other religions. Christian theodicy is also explicit in its exclusivity, and this provides unmatched precision and clarity for one who seeks deliverance from evil and suffering. Christ's sacrifice on the Cross and the actions of God objectively fulfilling His promises provide assurance of the elimination of evil. Finally, though God does not need human actions in order to accomplish His ultimate will or to defeat evil and end suffering, He invites believers to participate in His plans and to reap the resultant rewards. These particular aspects of mainstream Christian theodicy elevate it beyond mere sufficiency; they add to its compelling nature and desirability. This demonstrates the uniqueness of Christian theodicy, which is vital when one wishes to engage in productive interfaith dialogue.

CHAPTER 22:

Application, Next Steps, and Conclusion

THE PURPOSE OF THIS study is to establish a framework for effective interfaith dialogue about evil and suffering as well as to provide a paradigm for Christian theodicy that functions within the framework, while also providing evidence for its sufficiency and uniqueness in the context of interfaith dialogue. This study accomplished its purpose through achieving six objectives. First, the study critically examined existing works in the field of religious thought regarding evil. From those sources, it determined the individual definition of evil (or its equivalent) for each religion in such terms as to allow for comparative analysis. Second, it established the key questions and issues that each approach to evil and suffering addresses with regard to theological, philosophical, and experiential components. Third, using the findings from the previous chapters, it proposed a universal code of classification for religious thought about evil and suffering. Fourth, it classified the mainstream, major religious belief systems of Judaism, Christianity, Islam, Hinduism, and Buddhism according to the newly created universal code of classification. Fifth, the study demonstrated the sufficiency of mainstream Christian theodicy, with a focus on logical, historical, theological, and experiential consistency. Finally, the study proposed four key areas of Christian theodicy that make it unique and compelling in interfaith dialogue: historicity and valorization, assurance, exclusivity, and participation.

Exercising the Universal Code of Classification

The UCC provides an effective, balanced framework by which one may participate in or initiate interfaith dialogue on the topic of evil and suffering. It carefully represents the core parameters of each system of thought, and it allows for guided conversation about either the systems themselves or the particular doctrines of a system. The UCC maximizes portability and practical usefulness on account of its simple nature and low physical requirements (a writing utensil and something to write on is all that is required); however, its simplicity and portability do not undermine its potential for aiding in powerful discourse on the topic of evil. One need only illustrate the basic design and then the UCC is open and accessible for interaction involving people of all faiths, including those that this study did not investigate. The UCC's usefulness is potentially broad, and given the different opinions, perspectives, and approaches, one can use it in a variety of fashions within the context of interfaith dialogue. While far from exhaustive, some limited examples of expanded use follow.

Non-Apologetic Interfaith Dialogue

Specific to the topic of interfaith dialogue, use of the UCC can be of particular assistance when attempting to ensure understanding of different religious positions. While mainstream expressions of the faiths in this study match the plotted UCC positions provided earlier, it is useful to invite others who participate in the dialogue to plot their own positions on the UCC and explain why they plot them as they do. Also, it is useful to have others provide plots for their perception of the systems they do not adhere to. This provides a mechanism for exposing the delta between presuppositions and actualities with regard to the positions held by others, and use of this system can serve to focus dialogue along common topics. Interactive use of the UCC guides discussion along appropriate, topical commonalities, and it can spur additional conversation and understanding.

Christian Apologetic Dialogue

When the dialogue moves toward an apologetic approach, the UCC is particularly useful for careful, systemic apologetics. One does not need to start an apologetic conversation by exposing inconsistencies in the particular details of any specific theodicy. Rather, one can identify the overall system of evil that a religion employs, such as *hierodelusory/ arbitrary-anthroredemptive*. Then, one may engage in apologetic dialogue about any or all of the four main paradigms (axes, the common questions asked by each religion). The UCC provides a balanced and evenhanded format for apologetics focused on the underlying paradigms a particular theodicy employs. It provides further value and a proper frame of reference when the dialogue moves on to the particulars of a faith because it helps frame the particulars in the correct overall context.

Christian Polemical Dialogue

The UCC provides further value in the refutation of erroneous positions held by Christians with regard to theodicy (as well as related areas such as hamartiology, soteriology, and eschatology). By providing a systemic overview of all the possible variations, and by mapping an erroneous position along with the correct, orthodox, mainstream position, dialogue can ensue as to why there are several differences with regard to interpretation of theology, followed by focused, corrective discourse. Also of potential use is mapping the positions of other religions alongside the erroneous and correct positions in order to expose and explain undesirable syncretistic thought and similarities.

Suggestions for Further Research

The UCC succeeds in providing a framework for dialogue about evil and suffering, but its usefulness is not limited to the religions used in this study (the mainstream forms of Hinduism, Buddhism, Judaism, Christianity, and Islam). There are many ways to expand the usefulness of the UCC by combining it with additional research. The study designed the basic framework of the UCC to accept further data, revision, and application as part of its goal of extensibility.

The first logical extension of this research is to add other major religions to the UCC that are not part of the scope of this current study. Jainism, Sikhism, Zoroastrianism, Bahá'í, Taoism, Confucianism, and Secular Humanism are candidates for addition to the UCC via further research. Also, one could map various beliefs systems generally labelled as cultic (either alongside the religions or as a separate study), including New Age, Universal Unitarianism, Scientology, The Church of Jesus Christ of Latter-Day Saints, the Watchtower Bible and Tract Society, The International Society of Krishna Consciousness, and others.

The UCC could be useful for future intra-religion research. For example, one can use the UCC to diagram the variations within the multitude of different expressions of Buddhism. From the intra-religion, historical perspective, it is useful for historical data-mapping of positions held by a particular faith at different times in its history. Also, another variation would be to map the positions held by significant people (right or wrong) within the history of a particular religion (for example, historical theodicy as demonstrated by Luther, Aquinas, Arias, Origen, Pinnock, Barth, Augustine, etc.)

The UCC could also serve as part of extremely focused and specialized studies. For example, further research may use the UCC as part of cultural studies of particular regions. How do different religious groups within a specific region or culture vary in their ideas about evil and suffering? How do teens from the Unites States, Germany, Turkey, South Africa, the United Kingdom, and India define the proper system of evil? Given a user base in the hundreds of millions, how do popular video games portray evil and suffering? The future research that people can conduct using the UCC as a foundation is vast and varied.

Concluding Thoughts

Every major religion has either an explicit definition of evil or an implicit equivalent; there are no exceptions. While there exists much in the way of apologetics with regard to the overall topic of evil, much of it is ineffective without a common frame of reference. Sometimes authors lack basic understanding of different positions (leading to lots of straw-man attacks), and other times earnest interfaith dialogue suffers from a lack of shared interfaith terminology that is accurate and balanced.

The first concern of this study with regard to comparative theodicy was whether it is possible to discern and define the disparate approaches to evil in such a manner as to find truly equivalent concepts. The answer is an emphatic affirmative. There are topical equivalents in the areas of theological, philosophical, and experiential concern. Furthermore, the study demonstrated that it is possible to provide a superset of terminology that contains and communicates the entire variety of disparate views at a systemic level, while not sacrificing each religion's underlying precision for the sake of general, high-level, systemic dialogue.

Within the context of the UCC, mainstream Christian theodicy has a powerful argument for its sufficiency, particularly when considered alongside the systemic inconsistencies exposed in other theodicies. Furthermore, mainstream Christian theodicy possesses unique, particular attributes that elevate it beyond simple consistency and sufficiency. These special attributes make it highly compelling. Christian theodicy emphasizes a human existence that is real and valorized by God. Alone among the religions of the world, Christianity lays claim to a God who cares so deeply about the individuals of His creation that He became incarnate as one of them. While fully human, He remained fully God, and yet He did not avoid suffering or the experiences of evil. Rather, He bodily experienced life as a human would experience life, and His bodily sacrificial death and bodily resurrection are the only guarantee the world has of a future free from evil.

There are those who claim that theodicy may not be an appropriate topic for people to pursue (Wright, 2006:40). The claims are that finite people cannot know enough about God or fully comprehend the vast and intricate workings of the universe He created. Therefore, it is better to avoid the possibility, perhaps even the likelihood, of error in evaluating this area of theology. It is accurate to state that people are finite and limited in knowledge and comprehension. Paul was correct when he wrote, "for now we see in a mirror *dimly* . . . now I know *in part*" (1 Corinthians 13:12, emphasis added). However, a God who becomes incarnate and participates in a visible and meaningful fashion in people's lives is a God who expects people to investigate and evaluate the nature of His world and how He interacts with it. God does not tempt people to sin, yet He implicitly invites people into an exploration of His goodness and justice in the face of evil and suffering by nature of His physical, historical, objective actions. Therefore, it is neither sinful nor inappropriate for one to engage with this area of theology.

Regardless of minor variations within the mainstream Christian views of theodicy, Christianity's God does not originate or embrace evil. One ought not to view the continuing presence and prevalence of evil and suffering in the world as something that challenges the power and love of God. The evil that God will defeat is real. He dealt with humanity's sinfulness by providing a path for redemption. He creates value for His followers even in the darkest of times. God guarantees the defeat of evil in real, historical, objective, and personal time, and in doing so He gives humanity the only true hope for freedom from evil.

The prevalence of evil and suffering does not diminish the power and love of God. Rather, that God accomplishes His ultimate will in spite of evil and suffering is a great testimony to His true, complete, and unmatched sovereignty. The Christian system of evil is the only fully consistent, logical, and sufficient system of evil that is also unique in its value of humans and their physical existence, an existence that God valorized and will redeem as part of the final victory over evil.

Ὁ κύριός μου καὶ ὁ θεός μου

Bibliography

Al Faruqi, I. 1973. The Essence of Religious Experience in Islam. *Numen*, 20(3):186-201, Dec. Available: JStor. Date of access: 22 August 2007.

Al-Fayyumi, S. 1998. *The Book of Theodicy: A Translation and Commentary on the Book of Job*. Translated from the Arabic by L.E. Goodman. New Haven, CT: Yale University Press. 481p.

Albertini, T. 2003. The Seductiveness of Certainty: The Destruction of Islam's Intellectual Legacy by the Fundamentalists. *Philosophy East and West*, 53(4):455-470, Oct. Available: JStor. Date of access: 22 August 2007.

Alcorn, R. 2004. *Heaven*. Carol Stream, IL: Tyndale House Publishers, Inc. 533p.

Ali, M. 1990. *The Religion of Islam.* Dublin, OH: Ahmadiyya Anjuman Isha'at Islam. 617p.

Ali, M. 2008. *A Manual of Hadith.* Dublin, OH: Forgotten Books. 289p.

Allender, D. 2006. The Intersection of Character and Leadership. In The Leadership Summit's Top 10. The Top 10 Highest-Rated Leadership

Sessions of all Time. Barrington, IL: Willow Creek Association. [Audio lecture on CD.]

Althaus, P. 1966. *The Theology of Martin Luther*. Translated from the German by Robert Schultz. Philadelphia, PA: Fortress Press. 464p.

Aquinas, T. 1989. *Summa Theologiæ. A Concise Translation*. Notre Dame, IL: Ave Marie Press, Inc. 651p.

Ariel, D. 1995. *What Do Jews Believe? The Spiritual Foundations of Judaism*. New York, NY: Schocken Books. 290p.

Arkoun, M. 2003. Rethinking Islam. *Annals of the American Academy of Political and Social Science*, 588:18-39, Jul. Available: JStor. Date of access: 16 May 2008.

Arnold, C. 1996. Returning to the Domain of the Powers: "Stoicheia" as Evil Spirits in Galatians 4:3,9. *Novum Testamentum*, 38(1):55-76, Jan. Available: JStor. Date of access: 24 August 2007.

Asani, A. 2003. "So That You May Know One Another": A Muslim American Reflects on Pluralism and Islam. *Annals of the American Academy of Political and Social Science*, 588:40-51, Jul. Available: JStor. Date of access: 16 May 2008.

Augustine. 1961. *Confessions*. Translated by R.S. Pine-Coffin. London: Penguin Books. 347p.

Augustine. 1993. *The City of God*. New York, NY: The Modern Library. 892p.

Ben-Menahem, H. 2002. Maimonides on Equity: Reconsidering the "Guide for the Perplexed" III:34. *Journal of Law and Religion*, 17(1/2):19-48. Available: JStor. Date of access: 14 January 2008.

Benatar, D. 2002. Obligation, Motivation and Reward: An Analysis of a Talmudic Principle. *Journal of Law and Religion*, 17(1/2):1-17. Available: JStor. Date of access: 11 January 2008.

Betts, P. 2002. The New Fascination with Fascism: The Case of Nazi Modernism. *Journal of Contemporary History*, 37(4):541-558, Oct. Available: JStor. Date of access: 11 January 2008.

Bhagavad Gita. 2002. Translated from the Sanskrit by Stephen Mitchell. New York: Three Rivers Press. 223p.

Bible. 1999. The Zondervan New American Standard Study Bible. Grand Rapids, MI: Zondervan.

Birch, C. 2003. God of Compassion. In Neville, D. & Matthewes, P., *ed. Faith and Freedom. Christian Ethics in a Pluralist Culture*. Hindmarsh, Australia: ATF Press. p. 146-150.

Bilsky, L. 2001. Judging Evil in the Trial of Kastner. *Law and History Review*, 19(1):117-160, Spring. Available: JStor. Date of access: 11 January 2008.

Blythin, I. 1962: A Note on Genesis I 2. *Vetus Testamentum*, 12(1):120-121, Jan. Available: JStor. Date of access: 11 July 2007.

Bond, G. 1980. Therevada Buddhism's Meditations on Death and the Symbolism of Initiatory Death. *History of Religions*, 19(3):237-258, Feb. Available: JStor. Date of access: 10 September 2007.

Bonhoeffer, D. 1997. *Creation and Fall. Temptation*. New York, NY: Touchstone. 144p.

Boyd, G. 2003. *Is God to Blame?* Downers Grove, IL: InterVarsity Press. 211p.

Bradley, D. 1955. Religious Differences and the Study of Religions. *Journal of Bible and Religion*, 23(1):32-37, Jan. Available: JStor. Date of access: 21 August 2007.

Brener, A. 2004. *Mourning & Mitzvah: A Guided Journal for Walking the Mourner's Path Through Grief to Healing*. 2nd ed. Woodstock, VT: Jewish Lights Publishing. 259p.

Buddhadasa, B. 1989. Interfaith Understanding in the Buddhist-Christian Dialogue. *Buddhist-Christian Studies*, 9:233-235. Available: JStor. Date of access: 11 July 2007.

Buri, F. and Oliver, H. 1992. The True Self in the Buddhist Philosophy of the Kyoto School. *Buddhist-Christian Studies*, 12:83-102. Available: JStor. Date of access: 22 August 2007.

Burton, D. 2002. Knowledge and Liberation: Philosophical Ruminations on a Buddhist Conundrum. *Philosophy East and West*, 52(3):326-345, Jul. Available: JStor. Date of access: 2 January 2008.

Carmy, S. 1999. The Long and Winding Road: By Way of Introduction. In Carmy, S., *ed. Jewish Perspectives on the Experience of Suffering.* Northvale, NJ: Jason Aronson. p. 1-20.

Chaudhuri, H. 1954. The Concept of Brahman in Hindu Philosophy. *Philosophy East and West*, 4(1):47-66, Apr. Available: JStor. Date of access: 21 August 2008.

Chen, P. 2001. Sound and Emptiness: Music, Philosophy, and the Monastic Practice of Buddhist Doctrine. *History of Religions*, 41(1):24-48, Aug. Available: JStor. Date of access: 2 January 2008.

Chipman, L. 2001. Mythic Aspects of the Process of Adam's Creation in Judaism and Islam. *Studia Islamica*, 93:5-25. Available: JStor. Date of access: 11 January 2008.

Cho, S. 2002. The Rationalist Tendency in Modern Buddhist Scholarship: A Revaluation. *Philosophy East and West*, 52(4):426-440, Oct. Available: JStor. Date of access: 22 August 2007.

Chodron, P. 2000. *When Things Fall Apart: Heart Advice for Difficult Times.* Boston, MA: Shambhala Publications. 160p.

Clarke, S. 2002. Hindutva, Religious and Ethnocultural Minorities, and Indian-Christian Theology. *The Harvard Theological Review*, 95(2):197-226, Apr. Available: JStor. Date of access: 11 April 2008.

Clendenin, D. 1988. Security but not Certainty: Toward a Christian Theodicy. *Journal of the Evangelical Theological Society*. 31(1):321-328, Mar. Available: Libronix Digital Library System [CD].

Clendenin, D. 1992. God is Great, God is Good. Questions about Evil. *Ashland Theological Journal.* 24:35-48. Available: Libronix Digital Library System [CD].

Cleveland, W. and McGill, R. 1985. Graphical Perceptions and Graphical Methods for Analyzing Scientific Data. *Science*, 229(4716):828-833, Aug. Available: JStor. Date of access: 31 August 2008.

Cobb, J. 1977. Buddhist Emptiness and the Christian God. *Journal of the American Academy of Religion*, 45(1):11-25, Mar. Available: JStor. Date of access: 24 August 2007.

Cohen, A. 1995. *Everyman's Talmud: The Major Teachings of the Rabbinic Sages.* New York, NY: Schocken Books. 405p.

Cohen, A. 1996. Theology and Theodicy: On Reading Harold Kushner. *Modern Judaism*, 16(3):229-261, Oct. Available: JStor. Date of access: 11 July 2007.

Cohen, R. 2000. Kinsmen of the Son: Sakyabhiksus and the Institutionalization of the Bodhisattva Ideal. *History of Religions*, 40(1):1-31, Aug. Available: JStor. Date of access: 2 January 2008.

Craig, W. 2001. *Time and Eternity: Exploring God's Relationship to Time.* Wheaton, IL: Crossway Books. 272p.

Creel, A. 1972. *Dharma* as an Ethical Category Relating to Freedom and Responsibility. *Philosophy East and West*, 22(2):155-168, Apr. Available: JStor. Date of access: 21 August 2007.

Danheisser, R. 2003. Islam Compatible with Democracy, Not Monolithic, Muslim Panellists Say. *Washington File*: 9 September 2003. http://usembassymalaysia.org.my/wf/wf0909_islam.html. Date of access: 12 Feb. 2008.

Das, L.S. 1998. *Awakening the Buddha Within: Eight Steps to Enlightenment.* New York, NY: Broadway Books. 432p.

David, M. 2009. "The Correspondence Theory of Truth." In *The Stanford Encyclopedia of Philosophy*, ed. Edward N. Zalta. Available: http://plato.stanford.edu/entries/truth-correspondence. Date of access: 15 March 2010.

Davis, W. 1989. Buddhism and the Modernization of Japan. *History of Religions*, 28(4):304-339, May. Available: JStor. Date of access: 22 August 2007.

Deroche, M. 1992. Isaiah XLV 7 and the Creation of Chaos? *Vetus Testamentum*, 41(1):11-21, Jan. Available: JStor. Date of access: 11 July 2007.

Dillon, M. 2000. Dialogues with Death: The Last Days of Socrates and the Buddha. *Philosophy East and West*, 50(4):525-558, Oct. Available: JStor. Date of access: 2 January 2008.

Dowden, B. & Swartz, N. 2004. "Truth." In *Internet Encyclopedia of Philosophy*. Available: http://www.iep.utm.edu/truth/#H3. Date of access: 23 October 2009.

Dozeman, T. 2000. Masking Moses and Mosaic Authority in Torah. *Journal of Biblical Literature*, 119(1):21-45, Spring. Available: JStor. Date of access: 14 January 2008.

Eckardt, A. 1974. The Holocaust: Christian and Jewish Responses. *The Journal of Religion*, 67(1):453-454, Sep. Available: JStor. Date of access: 22 August 2007.

Eckel, M.D. 2003. "Buddhism." In Coogan, M., (ed.), *The Illustrated Guide to World Religions*. New York: OUP. p. 163-197.

Ehrlich, C.S. 2003. "Judaism." In Coogan, M., (ed.), *The Illustrated Guide to World Religions*. New York: OUP. p. 14-51.

El Fadl, K. 2001. Islam and the Theology of Power. *Middle East Report*, 221:28-33, Winter. Available: JStor. Date of access: 22 August 2007.

Eliade, M. 1957. *The Sacred and the Profane*. New York, NY: Harcourt, Inc. 256p.

Eliade, M. 1958. *Patterns in Comparative Religion*. Lincoln, NE: University of Nebraska Press. 484p.

Eliade, M. 1978. *A History of Religious Ideas: From the Stone Age to the Eleusinian Mysteries*. Chicago, IL: UCP. 479p.

Eliade, M. 1998. *Myth and Reality*. Long Grove, IL: Waveland Press, Inc. 204p.

Ellis, P. 1998. *The Ancient World of the Celts*. New York, NY: Barnes & Noble Books. 238p.

Elman, Y. 1990. The Suffering of the Righteous in Palestinian and Babylonian Sources. *The Jewish Quarterly Review*, 80(3/4):315-339, Jan.-Apr. Available: JStor. Date of access: 4 January 2008.

Engler, U. 2009. *History*. Universität Stuttgart. http://www.uni-stuttgart.de/ueberblick/geschichte/index.en.html. Date of access: 4 March 2010.

Erickson, M. 1998. *Christian Theology*. 2nd ed. Grand Rapids, MI: Baker Academic. 1,312p.

Eustace, H. 1999. *Christian Science: Its "Clear, Correct Teaching" and Complete Writings*. Berkeley, CA: Lederer, Street and Zeus Co. 1037p.

Fackenheim, E. 1982. The Spectrum of Resistance during the Holocaust: An Essay in Description and Definition. *Modern Judaism*, 2(2):113-130, May. Available: JStor. Date of access: 11 January 2008.

Fackenheim, E. 1985. The Holocaust and Philosophy. *The Journal of Philosophy*, 82(10):505-514, Oct. Available: JStor. Date of access: 4 January 2008.

Farah, C. 2003. *Islam*. Hauppauge, NY: Barron's Educational Series, Inc. 500p.

Feder, K. and Park, A. 1993. *Human Antiquity. An Introduction to Physical Anthropology and Archaeology*. 2nd ed. Mountain View, CA: Mayfield Publishing Company. 496p.

Feldman, L. 2000. Josephus' Portrayal (Antiquities 5.136-174) of the Benjaminite Affair of the Concubine and Its Repercussions (Judges 19-21). *The Jewish Quarterly Review*, 90(3/4):255-292, Jan.-Apr. Available: JStor. Date of access: 11 January 2008.

FEMA. 2006. Hurricane Katrina, One-Year Later. 22 Aug. 2006. http://www.fema.gov/news/newsrelease.fema?id=29108. Date of access: 27 Mar. 2010.

Fernandes, P. 2000. Opening Statement: Phil Fernandes. The Cumulative Case for God. (*in* Theism vs. Atheism. The Internet Debate. Bremerton, WA: IBD Press. p. 1-18).

Fernandes, P. 2002a. *The God Who Sits Enthroned: Evidence for God's Existence.* Fairfax, VA: Xulon Press. 180p.

Fernandes, P. 2002b. *No Other Gods: A Defense of Biblical Christianity.* Fairfax, VA: Xulon Press. 249p.

Fernandes, P. 2003. The Biblical Basis for Human Government. In *God, Government, and the Road to Tyranny*. Fairfax, VA: Xulon Press. p. 17-22.

Fernandes, P. 2009. *The Atheist Delusion: A Christian Response to Christopher Hitchens and Richard Dawkins*. Fairfax, VA: Xulon Press. 210p.

Fiddes, P. 1993. The Cross of Hosea Revisited: The Meaning of Suffering in the Book of Hosea. *Review and Expositor*, 90(2):175-188, Spring. Available: Libronix Digital Library System [CD].

Fingarette, H. 1984. Action and Suffering in the Bhagavadgita. *Philosophy East and West*, 34(4):357-369, Oct. Available: JStor. Date of access: 22 August 2007.

Fleming, D. 1994. Job: The Tale of Patient Faith and the Book of God's Dilemma. *Vetus Testamentum*, 44(4):468-482, Oct. Available: JStor. Date of access: 9 January 2008.

Flora, J. 1992. New Testament Perspectives on Evil. *Ashland Theological Journal.* 24:15-26. Available: Libronix Digital Library System [CD].

Fonner, M. 1993. Toward a Theravadin Christology. *Buddhist-Christian Studies*, 13:3-14. Available: JStor. Date of access: 22 August 2007.

Fox, D. 1971. Zen and Ethics: Dogen's Synthesis. *Philosophy East and West*, 21(1):33-41, Jan. Available: JStor. Date of access: 11 July 2007.

Frame, J. *No Other God. A Response to Open Theism*. Phillipsburg, NJ: P & R Publishing. 235p.

Frymer-Kensky, T. 1977. The Atrahasis Epic and Its Significance for Our Understanding of Genesis 1-9. *The Biblical Archaeologist*, 40(4):147-155, Dec. Available: JStor. Date of access: 22 August 2007.

Fundamental Articles of Faith. Islam 101. http://islam101.net/index.php?option=com_content&task=view&id=44&Itemid=32. Date of access: 7 July 2008.

Gardner, A. 1999. The Great Sea of Dan. VII 2. *Vetus Testamentum*, 49(3):412-415, Jul. Available: JStor. Date of access: 11 July 2007.

Geertz, C. 1971. *Islam Observed: Religious Development in Morocco and Indonesia*. Chicago, IL: UCP. 136p.

Geisler, N. 2001. *Chosen but Free*. Minneapolis, MN: Bethany House Publishers. 285p.

Geisler, N. 2002. *The Roots of Evil.* Eugene, OR: Wipf & Stock. 96p.

Geisler, N. 2004. *Systematic Theology. Volume 3. Sin. Salvation.* Minneapolis, MN: Bethany House. 624p.

Geisler, N. 2004. *Christian Apologetics*. Grand Rapids, MI: Baker Books. 390p.

Geisler, N. & Brooks, R. 1990. *Come Let us Reason*. Grand Rapids, MI: Baker Academic. 232p.

Geisler, N. & Corduan, W. 2003. *Philosophy of Religion*. Eugene, OR: Wipf and Stock Publishers. 302p.

Geisler, N. & Feinberg, P. 1987. *Introduction to Philosophy. A Christian Perspective*. Grand Rapids, MI: Baker Books. 447p.

Gethin, R. 1998. *The Foundations of Buddhism.* New York, NY: OUP. 333p.

Goleman, D. 2003. *Destructive Emotions: A Scientific Dialogue with the Dalai Lama.* New York, NY: Bantam. 404p.

Good, A. 2000. Congealing Divinity: Time, Worship and Kinship in South Indian Hinduism, *The Journal of the Royal Anthropological*

Institute, 6(2):273-292, Jun. Available: JStor. Date of access: 11 April 2008.

Goodman, L. 1998. Themes of Theodicy in the Exegesis of the Book of Job. Situating Saadiah's Reading in Its Historic and Philosophic Setting. In L. Goodman, *trans.*, *The Book of Theodicy: A Translation and Commentary on the Book of Job.* New Haven, CT: Yale University Press. p. 28-92.

Gordon, M. 2003. Islam. In Coogan, M., *ed. The Illustrated Guide to World Religions.* New York: OUP. p. 89-123.

Greene, V. 1992. "Accessories of Holiness": Defining Jewish Sacred Objects. *Journal of the American Institute for Conservation*, 31(1):31-39, Spring. Available: JStor. Date of access: 15 January 2008.

Grudem, W. 1994. *Systematic Theology*. Grand Rapids, MI: Zondervan. 1,290p.

Grunebaum, G. 1970. Observations on the Muslim Concept of Evil. *Studia Islamica*, 31:117-134. Available: JStor. Date of access: 11 July 2007.

Helseth, P. Open Theism and the Problem of Particular Evils. *Journal of the Evangelical Theological Society,* 44(3):493-511, Sep. Available: Libronix Digital Library System [CD].

Hendel, R. 1987. Of Demigods and the Deluge: Towards in Interpretation of Genesis 6:14. *Journal of Biblical Literature*, 106(1):13-26, Mar. Available: JStor. Date of access: 22 August 2007.

Henry, C. 1999. *God, Revelation and Authority. Volume VI: God Who Stands and Stays.* Wheaton, IL: Crossway Books. 535p.

Hershock, P. 2003. Renegade Emotion: Buddhist Precedents for Returning Rationality to the Heart. *Philosophy East and West*, 53(2):251-270, Apr. Available: JStor. Date of access: 2 January 2008.

Heschel, A. 1976. *God in Search of Man: A Philosophy of Judaism.* New York, NY: Farrar, Straus and Giroux. 437p.

Hines, T. 2003. The Atheistic Explanation for Evil: Houston, We Have a Problem. *Conservative Theological Journal.* 7(20):321-333, Mar. Available: Libronix Digital Library System [CD].

Houben, H. 2003. Southeast Asia and Islam. *Annals of the American Academy of Political and Social Science*, 588:149-170, Jul. Available: JStor. Date of access: 16 May 2008.

India. 1955. Hindu Marriage Act 25 of 1955. http://www.sudhirlaw.com/HMA55.htm. Date of access: 1 July 2009.

Ingersoll, R. 2000. What is Religion? In *Atheism. A Reader*. Amherst, NY: Prometheus Books. p. 78-86.

Isaacs, M. 2000. Suffering in the Lives of Christians: James 1:2-19a. *Review and Expositor*, 97(2):183-192, Spring. Available: Libronix Digital Library System [CD].

Janin, H. & Kahlmeyer, A. 2007. *Islamic Law: The Sharia from Muhammad's Time to the Present.* Jefferson, NC: McFarland & Company, Inc. 207p.

Jonas, H. 1987. The Concept of God after Auschwitz: A Jewish Voice. *The Journal of Religion*, 67(1):1-13, Jan. Available: JStor. Date of access: 22 August 2007.

Juynboll, G. 2001. (Re)Appraisal of Some Technical Terms in Hadith. *Islamic Law and Society*, 8(3):303-349. Available: JStor. Date of access: 16 May 2008.

Katz, N. 1995. The Judaisms of Kaifeng and Cochin: Parallel and Divergent Styles of Religious Acculturation. *Numen*, 42(2):118-140, May. Available: JStor. Date of access: 15 January 2008.

Keddie, N. 1963. Symbol and Sincerity in Islam. *Studia Islamica*, 19:27-63. Available: JStor. Date of access: 22 August 2007.

Keenan, J. 2002. A Mahayana Theology of Salvation History. *Buddhist-Christian Studies*, 22:139-147. Available: JStor. Date of access: 2 January 2008.

Keylor, W. 2008. "World War I." *Microsoft Encarta Online Encyclopedia 2008*. http://encarta.msn.com/encyclopedia_761569981_13/World_War_I.html. Date of access: 28 March 2009.

Kinnard, J. 1988. When Is The Buddha Not the Buddha? The Hindu/Buddhist Battle over Bodhgaya and Its Buddha Image. *Journal of the American Academy of Religion*, 66(4): 817-839, Winter. Available: JStor. Date of access: 21 August 2007.

Koran. 2004. The Koran. New York, NY: Bantam Dell.

Kronke, M. 2004. Evil in the Bible: A Theodicy of Relationship. M.A. Thesis, California State University Dominguez Hills, Carson, CA. 51p.

Kuhn, T. 1970. *The Structure of Scientific Revolutions*. 2nd ed. Chicago, IL: UCP. 210p.

Langermann, T. 2001. A Judaeo-Arabic Candle-Lighting Prayer. *The Jewish Quarterly Review*, 92(1/2):133-135, Jul.-Oct. Available: JStor. Date of access: 14 January 2008.

Lazarus-Yafeh, H. 1996. Some Neglected Aspects of Medieval Muslim Polemics against Christianity. *The Harvard Theological Review*, 89(1):61-84, Jan. Available: JStor. Date of access: 4 July 2008.

Leve, L. 2002. Subject, Selves, and the Politics of Personhood in Theravada Buddhism in Nepal. *The Journal of Asian Studies*, 61(3):833-860, Aug. Available: JStor. Date of access: 2 January 2008.

Levenson, J. 2000–2001. Religious Affirmation and Historical Criticism in Heschel's Biblical Interpretation. *AJS Review*, 25(1):25-44. Available: JStor. Date of access: 14 January 2008.

Lewis, CS. 2001. *A Grief Observed.* San Francisco, CA: HarperSanFrancisco. 76p.

Lichtenstein, A. 1999. The Duties of the Heart and Response to Suffering. In Carmy, S., *ed. Jewish Perspectives on the Experience of Suffering.* Northvale, NJ: Jason Aronson. p. 21-61.

Lorenzen, D. 1999. Who Invented Hinduism? *Comparative Studies in Society and History*, 41(4):630-659, Oct. Available: JStor. Date of access: 21 August 2007.

Lovell, F. 1955. Biblical and Classical Myths. *The Classical Journal*, 50(6):271-278+288, Mar. Available: JStor. Date of access: 22 August 2007.

Lytton, T. 2002-2003. "Shall Not the Judge of the Earth Deal Justly?": Accountability, Compassion, and Judicial Authority in the Biblical Story of Sodom and Gomorrah. *Journal of Law and Religion*, 18(1):31-55. Available: JStor. Date of access: 22 August 2007.

Majjhima-nikaya. Translated by Ñanamoli Thera & Bhikkhu Bodhi. http://www.accesstoinsight.org/tipitaka/mn/mn.009.ntbb.html. Date of access: 28 December 2007.

Makransky, J. 2000. Mahayana Buddhist Ritual and Ethical Activity in the World. *Buddhist-Christian Studies*, 20:54-59. Available: JStor. Date of access: 2 January 2008.

Major Sins, The. 2007. World of Islam. http://islam.worldofislam.info/index.php?option=com_content&task=view&id=659&Itemid=44. Date of access: 6 July 2008.

Major Sins in Islam, The. Brochure created and distributed by the Islamic Presentation and Invitation Center (IPIC). Seattle, WA: IPIC. (Copy of original in possession of study author.)

Marrus, M. 1987. Jewish Leaders and the Holocaust. *French Historical Studies*, 15(2):316-333, Autumn. Available: JStor. Date of access: 9 January 2008.

Martin, R. 1982. Understanding the Quran in Text and Context. *History of Religions*, 21(4):361-384. Available: JStor. Date of access: 11 July 2007.

Martin, W. 2003. *The Kingdom of the Cults*. Minneapolis, MN: Bethany House Publishers. 704p.

Mathewes, C. 2000. A Tale of Two Judgments: Bonhoeffer and Arendt on Evil, Understanding, and Limits, and the Limits of Understanding Evil. *The Journal of Religion*, 80(3):375-404, Jul. Available: JStor. Date of access: 11 January 2008.

McDowell, J. 1979. *Evidence that Demands a Verdict. Volume 1. Historical Evidences for the Christian Faith*. San Bernardino, CA: Here's Life Publishers, Inc. 397p.

McRobert, L. 1989. Emil L. Fackenheim and Radical Evil: Transcendent, Unsurpassable, Absolute. *Journal of the American Academy of Religion*, 57(2):325-340, Summer. Available: JStor. Date of access: 4 January 2008.

Meilaender, G. 2006. *The Freedom of a Christian*. Grand Rapids, MI: Brazos Press. 192p.

Metzger, B. 1994-1995. Revelation and Reason: A Dynamic Tension in Islamic Arbitrament. *Journal of Law and Religion*, 11(2):697-714. Available: JStor. Date of access: 22 August 2007.

Michaels, A. 2004. *Hinduism: Past and Present*. Translated by Barbara Harshaw. Princeton, NJ: PUP. 427p.

Miller, L. 2001. "Six Religions' Core View on God: A Search for Agreement and Accord." M.A. Thesis, California State University Dominguez Hills. 41p.

Mitchell, D. 2002. Concerning Ritual Practice and Ethics in Buddhism. *Buddhist-Christian Studies*, 20:84-89. Available: JStor. Date of access: 2 January 2008.

Moaddel, M. 2002. The Study of Islamic Culture and Politics: An Overview and Assessment. *Annual Review of Sociology*, 28:359-386. Available: JStor. Date of access: 16 May 2008.

Mohammad, N. 1985. The Doctrine of Jihad: An Introduction. *Journal of Law and Religion*, 3(2):381-397. Available: JStor. Date of access: 22 August 2007.

Moosa, E. 2000-2001. The Dilemma of Islamic Rights Schemes. *Journal of Law and Religion*, 15(1/2):185-215. Available: JStor. Date of access: 22 August 2007.

Moreland, J. 2003. *Scaling the Secular City*. Grand Rapids, MI: Baker Books. 275p.

Moreland, J. & Craig, W. 2003. *Philosophical Foundations for a Christian Worldview*. Downers Grove, IL: IVP. 654p.

Morgan, D. 2001. *The Best Guide to Eastern Philosophy and Religion*. New York, NY: Renaissance Books. 348p.

Mumisa, M. 2002. *Islamic Law: Theory & Interpretation*. Beltsville, MY: Amana Publications. 209p.

Murphy, F. 1986. Divine Plan, Human Plan: A Structuring Theme in Pseudo-Philo. *The Jewish Quarterly Review*, 77(1):5-14, Jul. Available: JStor. Date of access: 24 August 2008.

Narayanan, V. 2003. Hinduism. In Coogan, M., *ed. The Illustrated Guide to World Religions*. New York: OUP. pp. 126-161.

Nasr, S. 2002. *The Heart of Islam*. New York, NY: HarperSanFrancisco. 338p.

Nasr, S. 2003. *Islam: Religion, History, and Civilization*. New York, NY: HarperSanFrancisco. 198p.

Nath, V. 2001. From 'Brahmanism' to 'Hinduism': Negotiating the Myth of the Great Tradition. *Social Scientist*, 29(3/4):19-50, Mar. - Apr., Available: JStor. Date of access: 11 April 2008.

Nettler, R. 1994. A Modern Islamic Confession of Faith and Conception of Religion: Sayyid Qutb's Introduction to the Tafsir, fi Zilal al-Qur'an. *British Journal of Middle Eastern Studies,* 21(1):102-114. Available: JStor. Date of access: 22 August 2007.

Neusner, J. 1973. The Implications of the Holocaust. *The Journal of Religion*, 53(3):293-308, Jul. Available: JStor. Date of access: 22 August 2007.

Nietzsche, F. 1998. *Beyond Good and Evil.* Translated from the German by Marion Faber. New York, NY: OUP. 198pp.

Odell-Hein, E. 2007. "Christocentrism: Archaic Roots, Modern Meaning." M.A. Dissertation, Columbia Evangelical Seminary, Longview, WA. 136p.

Osborne, G. 1993. Theodicy in the Apocalypse. *Trinity Journal,* 14(1):63-77, Spring. Available: Libronix Digital Library System [CD].

Otto, R. 1958. *The Idea of the Holy.* Translated from the German by John Harvey. New York, NY: OUP. 232p.

Peters, R. & De Vries, G. 1976-1977. Apostasy in Islam. *Die Welt des Islams,* 17(1/4):1-25. Available: JStor. Date of access: 22 August 2007.

Perrett, R. 2002. Personal Identity, Minimalism, and Madhyamaka. *Philosophy East and West,* 52(3):373-385, Jul. Available: JStor. Date of access: 11 April 2008.

Phillips, W. 1991. The Problem of Evil: A Pastoral Approach. Part Two: The Good News. *Michigan Theological Journal,* 2(1):105-112, Spring. Available: Libronix Digital Library System [CD].

Pinnock. C. 1994. Systematic Theology. In *The Openness of God.* Downers Grove, IL: Intervarsity Press. p. 11-58.

Pinnock, C. 2001. *Most Moved Mover: A Theology of God's Openness.* Grand Rapids, MI: Baker Academic. 202p.

Prakash, B. 1955. The Hindu Philosophy of History. *Journal of the History of Ideas,* 16(4):494-505, Oct. Available: JStor. Date of access: 21 August 2007.

Radhakrishnan, S. & Moore, C.A. 1999. *A Sourcebook in Indian Philosophy.* Princeton, NJ: Princeton University Press. 683p.

Ram-Prasad, C. 2001. Saving the Self? Classical Hindu Theories of Consciousness and Contemporary Physicalism. *Philosophy East and*

West, 51(3):378-392, Jul. Available: JStor. Date of access: 2 January 2008.

Ramayana and Mahabharata. 2002. Translated from the Sanskrit by Romesh C. Dutt. Mineola, NY: Dover Publications, Inc. 333p.

Rao, K. 1970. On Truth: A Hindu Perspective. *Philosophy East and West*, 20(4):377-382, Oct. Available: JStor. Date of access: 21 August 2007.

Renard, J. 2002. *The Handy Religion Answer Book*. Canton, MI: Visible Ink Press. 582p.

Repentance for Major and Minor Sins. 2003. Islam Online http://www.islamonline.net/servlet/Satellite?pagename=IslamOnline-English-Ask_Scholar/FatwaE/FatwaE&cid=1119503547128. Date of access: 6 July 2008.

Reuters, 2010. Haiti death toll could reach 300,000, says Haitian President Rene Preval. 22 Feb. 2010. http://www.nydailynews.com/news/world/2010/02/22/2010-02-22_haiti_death_toll_could_reach_300000_says_haitian_president_rene_preval.html. Date of access: 27 Mar. 2010.

Rice, R. 1994. Biblical Support for a New Perspective. In *The Openness of God*. Downers Grove, IL: Intervarsity Press. p. 11-58.

Rig Veda. 1981. Translated from the Sanskrit by Wendy Doniger. New York: Penguin Books. 343p.

Rivers, D. 2009. Tsunami-battered countries restart, rebuild amid challenges. CNN. 23 Dec. 2009. http://www.cnn.com/2009/WORLD/asiapcf/12/22/tsunami.anniversary.rebuilding/index.html?iref=allsearch. Date of access: 27 Mar. 2010.

Roach, G & McNally, C. 2005. *The Essential Yoga Sutra: Ancient Wisdom for Your Yoga*. New York: Three Leaves Press. 108p.

Russell, B. 2000. Is There a God? In *Atheism. A Reader*. Amherst, NY: Prometheus Books. p. 87-94.

Russell, R. 1996. Redemptive Suffering and Paul's Thorn in the Flesh. *Journal of the Evangelical Theological Society*, 39(1):559-570, Mar. Available: Libronix Digital Library System [CD].

Rupp, G. 1971. The Relationship between Nirvana and *Samsara*: An Essay on the Evolution of Buddhist Ethics. *Philosophy East and West*, (21) 1:55-67, Jan. Available: JStor. Date of access: 11 July 2007.

Ryan, T. 2003. Catholic and Buddhist Monastics Focus on Suffering. *Buddhist-Christian Studies*, 23: 143-145. Available: JStor. Date of access: 2 January 2008.

Sandars, N. 1972. Introduction. In *The Epic of Gilgamesh*. Translated by NK Sandars. New York, NY: Penguin Books. p. 7-58.

Satlow, M. 2003. "And on the Earth You Shall Sleep": "Talmud Torah" and Rabbinic Asceticism. *The Journal of Religion*, 83(2):204-225, Apr. Available: JStor. Date of access: 15 January 2008.

Scarborough, M. 2000. In the Beginning: Hebrew God and Zen Nothingness. *Buddhist-Christian Studies*, 20:191-216. Available: JStor. Date of access: 2 January 2008.

Schaeffer, F. 1968. *Escape from Reason*. Downers Grove, IL: InterVarsity Press. 96p.

Schaeffer, F. 1998. *The Finished Work of Christ: The Truth of Romans 1 - 8*. Wheaton, IL: Crossway Books. 239p.

Scherman, N. & Zlotowitz, M. (eds). *The Chumash*. The Stone Edition. Brooklyn, NY: Mesorah Publications, Ltd. 1,313p.

Schiffman, L. 2000. The Dead Sea Scrolls and the History of Judaism. *Near Eastern Archaeology*, 63(3):154-159, Sep. Available: JStor. Date of access: 11 January 2008.

Schreiner, T. 1991. "Works of the Law" in Paul. *Novum Testamentum*, 33(3):217-244, Jul. Available: JStor. Date of access: 24 August 2007.

Seiichi, Y. 2001. The Distinction between Ego (e) and Ego-Self (e/S): Notes on Religious Practice Based upon Buddhist-Christian

Dialogue. *Buddhist-Christian Studies*, 21: 95-99. Available: JStor. Date of access: 2 January 2008.

Sharif, M. 1959. Islam and Spiritual Values. *Philosophy East and West*, 9(1/2):41-43, Apr-Jul. Available: JStor. Date of access: 22 August 2007.

Sharma, A. 2002. On Hindu, Hindustān, Hinduism and Hindutva. *Numen*, 49(1):1-36. Available: JStor. Date of access: 11 April 2008.

Shelly, P. 2000. A Refutation of Deism. In *Atheism. A Reader*. Amherst, NY: Prometheus Books. p. 69-77.

Shermer, M. 2004. *The Science of Good and Evil: Why People Cheat, Gossip, Care, Share, and Follow the Golden Rule.* New York, NY: Henry Holt and Company, LLC. 350pp.

Sheth, N. 2002. Hindu Avatāra and Christian Incarnation: A Comparison. *Philosophy East and West*, 52(1):98-125, Jan. Available: JStor. Date of access: 11 April 2008.

Shulman, D. 1979. Divine Order and Divine Evil in the Tamil Tale of Rama. *The Journal of Asian Studies*, 38(4):651-669, Aug. Available: JStor. Date of access: 11 July 2007.

Smart, N. 1984. Action and Suffering in the Theravadin Tradition. *Philosophy East and West*, 34(4):371-378, Oct. Available: JStor. Date of access: 22 Aug. 2007.

Smith, F. 2000. Indra Goes West: Report on a Vedic Soma Sacrifice in London in July 1996, *History of Religions*, 39(3):247-267, Feb. Available: JStor. Date of access: 11 April 2008.

Smith, H. 1991. *The World's Religions*. New York, NY: HarperCollins. 399p.

Sokol, M. 1999. Is There a "Halakhic" Response to the Problem of Evil? *The Harvard Theological Review*, 92(3):311-323, Jul. Available: JStor. Date of access: 4 January 2008.

Spero, S. 1986. Towards a Philosophy of Modern Orthodoxy. *Modern Judaism*, 6(1):79-90, Feb. Available: JStor. Date of access: 24 August 2007.

Stadler, N. 2002. Is Profane Work an Obstacle to Salvation? The Case of Ultra Orthodox (Haredi) Jews in Contemporary Israel. *Sociology of Religion*, 63(4):455-474, Winter. Available: JStor. Date of access: 11 January 2008.

Statement of Faith. 2008. Evangelical Free Church of America. http://www.efca.org/about-efca/statement-faith. Date of access: 7 January 2010.

Steinberg, M. 1975. *Basic Judaism*. New York, NY: Harcourt, Inc. 172p.

Steinmann, A. 1996. The Structure and Message of the Book of Job. *Vetus Testamentum*, 46(1):85-100, Jan. Available: JStor. Date of access: 9 January 2008.

Surin, K. 1983. Theodicy? *The Harvard Theological Review* 76(2):224-247, Jan. Available: JStor. Date of access: 22 August 2007.

Tanaka, K. 2002. Christian Prayer Seen from the Eye of a Buddhist. *Buddhist-Christian Studies*, 22:87-92. Available: JStor. Date of access: 2 January 2008.

Tukey, J. 1990. Data-Based Graphics: Visual Display in the Decades to Come. *Statistical Science*, 5(3):327-339, Aug. Available: JStor. Date of access: 31 August 2008.

United Kingdom. 1983. Mental Health Act 1983. Available: http://www.statutelaw.gov.uk/content.aspx?activeTextDocId=1729080. Date of access: 23 October 2009.

Upanishads. 1987. Translated from the Sanskrit by Eknath Easwaran. Tomales, CA: Nilgiri Press. 320p.

van Baaren, T. 2008. Monotheism. In Encyclopædia Britannica. http://www.britannica.com/EBchecked/topic/390101/monotheism. Date of access: 15 April 2008.

van der Veer, P. 2002. Religion in South Asia. *Annual Review of Anthropology*, 31:173-187. Available: JStor. Date of access: 11 April 2008.

van Inwagen, P. 1991. The Problem of Evil, The Problem of Air, and the Problem of Silence. *Philosophical Perspectives* 5:135-165. Available: JStor. Date of access: 22 August 2007.

Vogt, H. 2009. 2 Afghans Face Death over Translation of Quran. 6 Feb. 2009. http://news.yahoo.com/s/ap/20090206/ap_on_re_as/as_afghan_translation_on_trial. Date of access: 6 Feb. 2009.

Wainer, H. 1984. How to Display Data Badly. *The American Statistician*, 38(2):137-147, May. Available: JStor. Date of access: 31 August 2008.

Wainwright, W. 2005. Monotheism. In The Stanford Encyclopedia of Philosophy. http://plato.stanford.edu/entries/monotheism/. Date of access: 15 April 2008.

Wald, K. & Martinez, M. 2001. Jewish Religiosity and Political Attitudes in the United States and Israel. *Political Behavior*, 23(4):377-397, Dec. Available: JStor. Date of access: 11 January 2008.

Walston, R. 2007. Is Hinduism Monotheistic? http://www.columbiaseminary.edu/coffeetalk/122.html. Date of access: 5 May 2008.

Ware, B. 2000. *God's Lesser Glory: The Diminished God of Open Theism*. Wheaton, IL: Crossway Books. 240p.

Watt, W. 1979. Suffering in Sunnite Islam. *Studia Islamica*, 50:5-19. Available: JStor. Date of access: 11 July 2007.

Wayman, A. 1957. The Concept of Poison in Buddhism. *Oriens*, 10(1):107-109, July. Available: JStor. Date of access: 21 August 2007.

Weatherhead, L. 1972. *The Will of God*. Nashville, TN: Abingdon Press. 86p.

What are the Major Sins? 2003. Islam Online http://www.islamonline.net/servlet/Satellite?pagename=IslamOnline-English-Ask_Scholar/FatwaE/FatwaE&cid=1119503547542. Date of access: 6 July 2008.

White, J. 2000. *The Potter's Freedom: A Defense of the Reformation and the Rebuttal of Norman Geisler's Chosen But Free*. Merrick, NY: Calvary Press Publishing. 338p.

Williamson, C. 1983. Things Do Go Wrong (And Right). *The Journal of Religion*. 63(1):44-56, Jan. Available: JStor. Date of access: 24 August 2007.

Wright, N.T. 2003. *The Resurrection of the Son of God.* Minneapolis, MN: Fortress Press. 817p.

Wright, N.T. 2006. *Evil and the Justice of God.* Downers Grove, IL: IVP. 176p.

Yinger, J. 1977. A Comparative Study of the Substructures of Religion. *Journal for the Scientific Study of Religion*, 16(1):67-86, Mar. Available: JStor. Date of access: 31 August 2008.

Zacharias, R. 2000. *Jesus Among Other Gods: The Absolute Claims of the Christian Message*. Nashville, TN: W Publishing Group. 195p.

Ziemke, E. 2008. World War II. *Microsoft Encarta Online Encyclopaedia 2008*. http://encarta.msn.com/encyclopedia_761563737_15/World_War_II.html. Date of access: 28 March 2009.

About the Author

ERIC ODELL-HEIN IS THE president of Columbia Evangelical Seminary, a seminary where the ministry focus is meeting the educational needs of those who do not have easy access to a local seminary education. He earned a bachelor of theology, a master of religious studies in world religions, a master of divinity in practical theology, and a PhD in theology with a study emphasis on comparative theodicy. Coming from a varied church background, he has been serving at the Summit Evangelical Free Church in Enumclaw, Washington since 2002, where he is currently the teaching pastor. He has also spent significant time working in the technology industry, with most of his time in that industry focused on the area of gaming.

Eric lives in the Pacific Northwest with his wife, Christine, and they recently celebrated their twenty-fifth anniversary. They adopted their son, Ephraim, in 2008. In Eric's spare time, he enjoys travel, reading, theological conversations, and video games. His favorite activity is to connect with friends and discuss life and God.

Order Information

To order additional copies of this book, please visit
www.redemption-press.com.
Also available on Amazon.com and BarnesandNoble.com
Or by calling toll free 1-844-2REDEEM.

CPSIA information can be obtained
at www.ICGtesting.com
Printed in the USA
FFOW04n1949211117
43682545-42528FF